THE LIFE AND TIMES OF
DR. MAXIMUS SCHWANTZ
AKA DR. MICHAEL SWANK

DR. MICHAEL SWANK

Palmetto Publishing Group
Charleston, SC

The Life and Times of Dr. Maximus Schwantz Aka Dr. Michael Swank
Copyright © 2019 by Dr. Michael Swank

All rights reserved
No portion of this book may be reproduced, stored in a retrieval system, or transmitted in any form by any means–electronic, mechanical, photocopy, recording, or other–except for brief quotations in printed reviews, without prior permission of the author.

First Edition

Printed in the United States

ISBN-13: 978-1-64111-350-2
ISBN-10: 1-64111-350-2

INTRODUCTION

This memoir is dedicated to the many incredible physicians, nurses and allied health professionals with whom I came in contact with over 48 years. Everyone in the book is or were real and are represented by initials or first name. I did not use fictitious names as most people can easily be identified by a careful Google search. I apologize in advance if anyone is offended in any manner by my representation of them.

The stories in the book reflect the author's recollection of events. The places are real. The dialogue has been recreated from memory to be as correct as possible. The author has been careful not to disclose the present locations of anyone so as to protect their privacy.

In late March of 2018 I sat down with pen in hand under a beautiful Colorado sky looking West to the Rockies and began to record my Life leading to and entering the world of Medicine and Surgery. This is my story of highs and lows, good times and bad and adventures on the way. It begins. The Title is from my Nickname picked up in the Operating Room. Michael Swank MD.

FORWARD

Brothers, what we do in life…echoes in eternity.

*General Maximus Decimus
Meridius in Gladiator*

I was born on the 13th of November in 1945 in a small coal mining town 90 miles Northwest of Philadelphia with one brother in the household, nine years older, and a sister followed in a year and a half. My father was a school teacher (biology) and mother a registered nurse. I was named Michael because my birth happened around St. Michael's day in the Eastern Rite Catholic church. My mom told me when I was around ten that a nurse told her that I was one of the ugliest babies born in the hospital. I did see pictures and I agree but it got a little better as time went on.

Between 1945 and 1956, from birth to age 11, we lived in Gilberton, PA. The town had maybe 800 people in the area, a paved road out front and a dirt road behind until about '53 or '54 when it got paved. Everyone knew everyone and cared for each other. Every Saturday from April to October many people on back street where we lived came to a large yard for dinner where there was an outdoor wood fire.

Father taught school and, in the summers, sold cars, did retail at a soft pretzel shop and custard stand. My sister and I helped. Mother worked until I was eight or nine then became a wonderful homemaker. We had a small house which had two bedrooms and was heated by a coal stove. We cooked on a coal stove and we did have an indoor bathroom shared with my aunt and uncle next door. Summers I helped grandfather in his private, small coal mine but more lucrative was a bunch of us stealing the coal in coal cars lined up at night and selling the cracked coal for use in home cooking stoves. It was a great plan we had, and we carried it out never getting caught, usually on Friday's when all the workers were at the bars.

All of us kids played games in the street such as kick the can, hide and seek and bull in the middle. We hung out, I learned a lot about life and a little about sex. Back then, the usual line was "I'll show you mine if you show me yours." Which was strange stuff at 10 and 11!! We camped in the surrounding foothills of the Appalachian Mountains. We were unafraid and explored a lot.

Loved to watch the only policeman we had flag down cars speeding on Main Street and the fun when they would not stop! Finally got a police car!

A tragedy to remember was the death of my friend Eugene from complications of Polio! Thank God that is all gone for years now. I remember visiting him when things got bad and he was in the Iron Lung machine. I will never forget that day. Never wanted to see that again. He fought and fought, and we played when we could. His passing at age seven or eight affected our little town very much. I thought that the damn virus would outgrow him or vice versa. It did not. The Sauk Polio vaccine saved us.

My school had two buildings with grades one through eight in one building, four rooms, two grades per room heated by a coal stove in the center. High school was 20 yards above. Everything was postage size. I remember watching my brother play basketball in the smallest gym I have ever seen. Also, watched all the World Series games there on a TV, all day games. Started just after Labor Day and you watched when you had the time. This included epic games of the Dodgers vs. Yankees. Brooklyn was my team!

I remember my first day of school, first grade, got there and immediately ran away as fast as I could. A posse of 8th graders ran me down in less than an hour and I was carted back! I was going to try it again on Day 2 but then I thought it would be a repeat and my parents would not be happy.

Grade School (Gilberton highlights) -

1. Great fight with a guy named John in 5th grade at recess. Told me I looked like a girl and should wear a skirt. Students circled, and we fought bare knuckles. Ended up a draw with bloody noses but I thought I won because he lost two teeth! Never bothered me again.

2. Only had one janitor so we students had to help putting out the flag, hauling coal in buckets to each room and cleaning up. No complaints, just did it except one time I spilled a bucket of coal on the steps and had to clean it up piece by piece. We should have brought the coal we stole to school!

3. Remember like yesterday – summer sleep over by my sister's friend Eileen. We were 10 but she was tall with raven hair and eyes that made her seem older and more mature. She had an authority about her that she was in command. It was different. She asked if we could be with each other without our clothes and of course I said yes! We did a little touching but that was all. She liked what happened with my penis!

4. Sports – Nothing organized but we had baseball and football teams coached by dads (my dad did a lot as he played football for a team that became the New York Giants). We walked 2-3 miles to play other teams in other small towns. Those were great times! Everyone got along great. I look back and am amazed how organized we all were.

Summers were different in that only afternoons and early evening was available for play as for eight weeks we had four hours Monday through Friday with the nuns at school for religious instruction.

They were tough. They rapped your knuckles with heavy rulers for even minimal non-attentiveness. Also, we were Ukrainian Eastern Rite Catholic and went to church every Sunday unless sick - plus 51 holy days!! My mom got us there for almost each one! So, for 13 years, I spent about two hours of 103 days per year so 206 hours per years times 13 years = wow 2678 hours!! And when I was 35, mom said I was still paying for my sins!!

Otherwise summer was play, chores, working the custard stand or pretzel shop and learning about girls starting around age nine and starting just after dark.

Occasionally we left town for two-day trips to the Jersey shore, picnics and swimming at my aunt's farm, a trip to Washington D.C., Gettysburg, New York. Washington was awesome with the buildings and sense of power, but two things really struck me most: the majesty of the Lincoln Memorial and the profound sense of both sadness, honor and thanks felt at Arlington National Cemetery. To this day, each time I am there, the parting words of General MacArthur ring out – "Duty, Honor, Country". Gettysburg was a lesson in incredible bravery and sacrifice in the face of decisions both good and bad by both sides in our horrible Civil War. Everyone should go there to walk the fields where fate allowed our country to become whole again. On my initial visit to New York I loved the Concrete Canyons, the number of people from many places, the thought of all the power and the feeling of awe at the top of the Empire State Building.

One crazy thing we did in summer – North of town was the landfill dump and we would sit up on the hill with our 22 rifles and shoot at rats!! You don't see that in the suburbs!!

Highlight of winters – Finally getting a TV in '52 or '53 but there wasn't much on. Superman and cartoons I remember, early western stuff and nightly news. The sheer amount of snow I remember in a secluded small-town necessitated 'neighbors helping neighbors' – we had no plow trucks or snow blowers, just man power. But everyone pitched in to help each other and we all got to work and school. We had one long hill for sledding but a bit dangerous as the main road was at the bottom. Bobby R. one time slid right under a semi! Thought he bought the ranch, but he was Irish! Crazy chances we took sometimes but we lived, except Eugene who had no luck at all.

We were a small town in which everyone trusted and watched over one another. We learned, played and grew.

Also, I learned I had to be a doctor. Influences, feelings, etc.

1. The death of Eugene – could I have helped in some way? Or a grown up? Or some other doctors in a large city?

2. Just always had a feeling of wanting to help people, later it extended to girls but that was sexual, I think.

3. One day I found a dead mouse at about age eight. Borrowed my father's biology dissecting kit and started exploring the insides of the mouse. I was fascinated!

4. I had warts on the backs of my hands one summer. My grandmother told me to cut a potato in half and rub it all over my hands, don't wash and then bury the potato in the backyard. It worked! They disappeared. Must have been something in the raw potato or just luck but either way it got me curious.

5. Also, Eileen was very forward and invited me to explore a girl's anatomy and vice versa. It certainly piqued my interest in anatomy!

6. Going through my dad's biology books, etc. As I moved through my teens my mind was never focused on anything other than medicine, so I was chosen!

Secretly I admit that I really also thought about being a Marine – best uniforms, elite, tough, fit – all of the things a girl would like!

My fantasy job based on what has gone on in the world in the 60's, 70's and beyond:

- A major arms dealer (guns, etc.) – plan: learn French, Spanish, Chinese, etc.

- Join the Marine's and learn to survive and kill, etc.

- Get to Marseilles France to begin with a job and finding out all about the military trading/dealing

...and if I got really lucky and stayed alive, I could have retired at 50 with a few million dollars and a great woman (or two) to the wild coast of South Africa! Instead, I opted to be a surgeon!

1957 – 1963 relocation, change and high school: The winter (early spring) of 1957 brought changes to the household. My older brother returned from the military having served in the 11 Airborne Division, and when he still balked at going to college my dad got him a job with a friend's construction company and Pete was given the dirtiest, worse job. After three weeks he was applying to college on the GI Bill. My dad announced his appointment as supervising principal in another school district and in addition a planned move to a better home and a better long-term school up the mountain in Frackville, PA. My sister and I would be just three blocks from the middle (6, 7 and 8th grade) & high school and have a chance at organized sports and activities.

So, after finishing the 6th grade I was now ready for another adventure keeping my goal of being a surgeon in mind. That summer of '57 introduced me to organized baseball with the little league. My only one at age 12. I was assigned a team who, it turned out, needed a catcher (no one wanted the job). I got elected because I was the "new kid". It was a good summer of fun, getting used to the new house and new friends. I remember I hit only one home run in baseball and my parents were there to see it. It came with free ice cream afterwards.

Fall brought school and introduction to my class of 1963, about 75 kids. Classes were just up the hill from the high school and enjoyable as I remember 7th and 8th grades. The best times I had during this part of life was playing midget football in the fall of '57 and '58. We were relatively organized with coaches and practices and I was excited these two friends of mine from the valley were able to play with us. It is interesting in that from this obscure group of 20 – 25 kids in the Appalachian Mountains of PA, six went on to play later in college (Rutgers, Kent State, Penn State, Cornell, Bloomsburg, Kutztown).

The most memorable game played was before the inmates at the state penitentiary in Lewisburg against a local team. We all were a little scared at first, but it turned out to be an amazing experience with the inmates cheering and taking sides. We won the game! The most fun we had was on the bus to the games where we hung out the window our tallest guy Hal (Ducky) to see if he could gently give a butt tap to any girl riding a bike. Just think where that would get us today! And no one brought charges after 10 – 20 years!

Another great time was the summer of 1958 when a group of guys I started to pal around with would get together from things like tennis to visits to each other's houses and spending time camping in the surrounding mountains. We began friendships that have lasted a lifetime and the experiences we had were forever memorable and sometimes embellished through the years.

Academics were easy for me and I do not remember any areas of concern but always kept in the back of my mind that if I wanted to get to medical school so far all was small potatoes.

As far as girls were concerned, I remember this time, as they were only a mild curiosity in my life because of all the other activity. Real sexual awakenings began a bit later for me but when it happened, it exploded.

1959 – 1963 High School years in a small town – I suppose that our teenage years in a small town of 5,000 in Pennsylvania with no racial, cultural or technological diversity might be just plain ordinary. Far from it as we were surprisingly well aware of all that went on out of our radius of life; the rise of rock and roll and country music, the civil rights movement, the closest Presidential election to date (1960), the Cuban Missile crisis and the beginnings of he Vietnam War, to name a few.

High school was all in one building fairly central in the town to which almost everyone walked, went home for lunch, started at 8:30 AM and ended at 3:36 PM, never had a snow day or protests or walkouts. The teachers were adequate and fair but not outstanding as I remember with the toughest classes being physics and advanced math.

I formed a close-knit group with eight guys (one from a private school) and three girls around me and we did most things together along with other classmates. We helped each other with classwork and understanding the work. I got help with advanced calculus for instance and helped out with Latin which I seemed to have an affinity for. I also helped with history which I began to develop a real love for.

We did sports together with myself doing four years of football, two years of Junior Varsity basketball and two years of track and field. It was tough being a small school as many times we went up against larger schools but always did our best to meet all challenges. There were some quirky, funny and thoughtful things we did highlighted here:

1. One night we burned the eight-man football blocking sled in the middle of the field as we were sick of it only to have it appear new in a week!

2. I could not ride the bus to games without throwing up when we got there so the guys had bets on how soon and where it would occur. Then all was okay and off to play.

3. I threw the javelin in the field events and one practice got off a great throw. My teammate ran with the flight path not away from it. The javelin caught him right in his butt taking out a small chunk with no great harm, except, the guys put up a small plaque citing "My First Piece of Ass".

4. Freshman and Sophomore year having to play Junior Varsity football on Monday then Friday or Saturday Varsity football since we had so few players. One time we played a larger school taking 12 guys with one breaking his thumb on kickoff and the rest of us playing both ways for the entire game. We lost!

5. Interesting for me, my father, even though he played college football at St. Francis and some early pro ball, never went to any of our games. I don't remember ever talking with him about that even though it seems I should have and wish I did. It never impacted my play and I never felt anger towards him. Perhaps because a bad knee injury from football which kept

him out of the military when he wanted to serve his country curbed his interest. Still remains a mystery to me today.

6. I was recruited by Brown University and Princeton to play football for them but because there is a "no scholarships" rule at Ivy League schools I could not afford the cost, nor did I think that working two jobs, playing football and studying pre-med would let me make it through. Hard to take but was a wise choice. My good friend Frank W went with another guy to University of Kentucky to interview but quickly left when guys started talking about sexual encounters with chickens! We never knew the truth!

The social aspect of high school outside of sports was our sexual awakening with girls and the pursuit of all things adult and sexual. Because the drinking age was 21 in Pennsylvania and a false ID almost impossible to get. Parties were the norm at various homes when parents were out or away or sometimes looked the other way. Beer and some cigarettes were consumed but I remember very little liquor. In the summers we had big time players come to a venue in our county. We saw Elvis, Chubby Checker, the Everly Brothers and Buddy Holly to name but a few. There were also local dances with local bands and trips to the Jersey shore where some girls from our class worked and we visited. Where "Jersey girls" were quite "hospitable".

Lots of good times and make out sessions were held by everyone. But I believe that only one of my close friends and perhaps a classmate or two every actually had sexual intercourse. You may not believe this, but I knew girls who pinned their blouses to their underpants as "protection" from "going to far".

There was always lots of talk on breast comparison and who had the best legs (lots of girls wore shorter black skirts) and whose hair was the finest. It seemed like we all loved the exploration and the chase. Never getting to the ultimate sexual experience in high school did not really matter. It was the chase that was important!

Other neat and interesting things for me: getting picked up for school by my friend Bob in his new '64 Mustang convertible, as a senior going to some speakeasys which sprung up around the county, having a close girlfriend for a while to talk a lot, hang out, and dream – and take advantage of her father's grocery store! I got to feed my thirst for history with visits to places like Valley Forge, Gettysburg, West Point and Washington DC during those four years. The forming of close bonds with people who I have remained close to now for 56 odd years, mourning two who are no longer with us.

The first really national scare of our lives was the Cuban Missile Crisis. This got our attention because it involved the first big confrontation of two nuclear powers and a young, untested President sparring with a tough Soviet dictator. I remember watching everything I could on television wondering all the time whether my generation would be launched into something the world never wanted to see. We all breathed a sigh of relief one afternoon when the Russians blinked – and the whole world felt a great weight lifted. The fact that we could bet on college football in school on Thursday afternoons. FUN! Marrones pizza on Fridays after football, beers at Gravel Gurthie's, The Coal Bin Lounge (speakeasy) and out of bags at safe places and cars.

Helping out neighbors with the tons of snow we got. Late Sunday mornings at Catholic Mass at St. Joe's with "Father Fast", 20 minutes flat in Latin.

Christmas time at the Russian Orthodox friendly club with no collusion or election tampering. Caroling, pretending we know Russian always getting a shot and a beer.

Writing the word "futz" on school buildings in protest never even knowing what it meant. Running the concession stand at the community pool one summer led me to never consider being a fast food manager.

Gas was $.22 a gallon, movies $.50 - $1.00 and food and beer were cheap.

All seemed to flow as easy as a stream in summer.

At June graduation realizing that now the rubber meets the road in college, game on, academics get tougher so keep your eye on a medical degree and all else comes after that effort. If college plans failed, I would join the Marines, try for OC school and see where it took me.

College Years September 1963-May 1966 - After graduation celebrations settled into history and our group decided on various colleges or work, we set off to make our marks but no more than five hours from our homes. We all know we would see each other at some holidays. To save money and to help at home I decided to attend Penn State University for a year nearby in Pottsville before going to the main campus at State College. Thus, my graduation present was my first car mainly for the commute. It was a used 1959 Studebaker Lark with NO frills and lots of jokes made about it.

The summer of 1963 was spent working in a local factory for $1.10 per hour, getting ready for college and having our last fling at the Jersey shore and local joints. Best memory was being introduced to AP a senior to be at a rival school who was a beautiful blonde with a husky, sexy voice who smoked Newport light cigarettes and had a knock out smile. We hit it off well and more on that as the frost was getting on the pumpkin. It was an interesting year with a tough pre-med curriculum, commuting sometimes in bad weather down a winding mountain road to the college about 14 miles from home.

Great bunch of classmates mostly all local and salt of the earth. The only thing different than the usual classes was mandatory ROTC (Reserve Officer Training Program) since we were a state university. Somehow, I made it to command of the company by vote of my peers, but my proudest deed was the ability to field strip an M1 Garand rifle and put it back together! I was also elected Class President after a few weeks in order to deal with any problems with the Administration of which there were none.

My most vivid memory of the fall quarter was November 22nd, 1963, late morning. I was exiting English Literature class when a friend grabbed me and told me of the assassination of President Kennedy a short time ago. We gathered at the small student union around the television. Everyone was quiet, some sobbing, others just sitting in disbelief. Classes remaining for the day were canceled and we had the longest ride home that I can remember. "Why" was the looming question and there was no answer. More questions arose when I, as many others did, watched Jack Ruby kill Lee Harvey Oswald (JFK's suspected assassin) on live television. The world truly had turned upside down.

Years later I visited Dallas and spent a long time at the assassination site. I left with a firm thought and a good question which lingers today. There could well have been two shooters and why could not one of several qualified marksmen reproduce the shooting with the rifle Oswald used? One interesting small fact I will share from an excellent source…when Mrs. Kennedy came into the trauma room when the President was declared dead and all but two persons were left, she removed his wedding ring, put it on her hand and simply said, "Got a cigarette?" and walked out after it was lit for her.

Fall of '63 – May '64 was generally filled with hard work with college and little time for down time or partying. AP, now a senior in high school was my escape and adventure. Just before I was 18 she introduced me to sexual intercourse with knowledge and ease in a comfortable environment in her home absent her parents. That great experience set into motion a need I have loved, sometimes avoided, took selfishly and struggled to dismiss, sometimes failing badly. We had many good times and really enjoyed each other until she went off to Catholic University in Washington DC the summer of '64 and I went to work in New Jersey for college funds.

From the summer of 1964 until July of 1966 events occurred either at the Penn State campus in State College, PA or Northern New Jersey, New York City and my home area of PA. Thus, I will break them up.

My brother had a teaching job in northern New Jersey and worked for Johns Manville Corporation in the summer. So, after I successfully completed my first year of Pre-Med with good grades, I took his advice and initially spent days in the JM employment office until they got sick of me and gave me a job. My title was "sweeper" which meant cleaning and sweeping the working production areas and the bathrooms and showers. I was assigned to the rubber compound areas where it smelled and was always dirty.

I was taken under wing by a fellow guy from Jersey named Ronnie who said, "Kid, you seem smart. Let me show you how the boss will think you are doing the most work yet actually very little. Then you will get a better job next summer." We did just that. As an example, July 4th when we volunteered for double time and a half pay. We worked about two hours and played cards for six. Ronnie was a master showman! But the work got done and next summer I progressed.

I learned a lot about the life of a blue-collar worker those two summers ('64 and '65) and it taught me a lot about life. One summer I lived with my brother and his wife and the next with two other workers nearby.

I got along with almost everyone at work, partly, I believe, because I was called upon as "the college kid" to solve disputes of who was right about what and everyone accepted my analysis. Many times, I just dazzled them with bullshit!!

The guys took me to a number of typical New Jersey roadhouses in addition to the club that the company had for employees. There were lots of women, lots of hard drinking and living. I met a secretary who was a cut above the average in every way and we did have some good times. Roadhouses were the good, the bad and the ugly. It was great to witness blue collar interactions in an interesting culture. The quest for women and sometimes fights, nasty people tossed out and one ugly night when shots were fired, and I crawled out back of the place and walked five miles home. My reflections later about life in the "blue collar world" are that 1. Those people were a big part of the fabric of America. 2. They were mostly good people who worked hard for their families, loved their country and protected each other. 3. They also played hard, drank sometimes a little too much and were not kind to people of "other sexual orientation". This all taught me to respect all people, see life from their point of view, simply ignore what is impossible to change and move on.

Since I had my little car I did get back home for visits with friends and twice with AP for crazy good sex. New York City was an easy ride through the Lincoln Tunnel, park at the Port Authority and ride the subway anywhere. I went to the World's Fair, saw Broadway shows for as little as $8.00, loved the delis, all the sites and the excitement of the Concrete Canyons. I fell in love with NYC! The World's Fair in 1964-65 was an amazing array of pavilions from many countries showcasing their culture. The most memorable for me was the Spanish production. I sat in complete awe of the Flamenco dancers – they were beautiful, athletic and perfectly performed such exotic dance moves.

As August of 1964 approached, I accepted an invitation from Phi Sigma Kappa at Penn State in State College, invited by my good friend Frank. It was an opportunity extended to certain people from the campus extensions to stay at the fraternity house and have a good chance at becoming a Brother. It turned out to be great for me.

So, after nine to ten weeks of working and my Studebaker Lark now dead on arrival back home, my dad drove me the two and a half hours to 501 Allen Street in State College. There I settled in and began another interesting year.

I decided to take a shot at walking on with the football team and made it to the practice squad with the opportunity to possibly suit up for home games in the fall and the next season. Total games were six over two years with maybe 90 seconds of playing time. College sports were so different back then; people were smaller, steroids and growth hormones nonexistent, no big emphasis on weight lifting, stadiums were smaller (PSU had 48,000 seats). Overall it was only one small part of a large experience for me as I navigated a new environment and began to hone in on the quest for medical school.

I fit in well at Phi Sig. The house was in fine shape. The guys were all great and the history and traditions were excellent. Of the fraternities Phi Sigma Kappa was always in the top five in academics and intramural sports within the frat system. I was asked to become a pledge in a class of five great guys. It was obvious we were all picked for at least a good measure of academic prowess and athletic ability to some degree.

Our pledge class worked hard carrying out all of our duties which were many such as cleaning in general and after parties and events, preparing meals on weekends, wake up calls, one big project for the house and other general chores.

We did, however, have a few "ringers" in the sports competition, for example, John J was the National Badminton champion and Frank Z, a receiver in flag football was the fastest sprinter on the Penn State track team.

That fall and through the time I became a Brother in early spring was tough. Academic, football, intramurals and pledge duties did not allow much time for anything else. AP did get up for a couple of parties from Washington but after that things began to cool down with us as the distance took its toll. A good month off for Christmas at home after a successful GPA (Grade Point Average) was nice. I saw my old friends a number of times, met new ones and relaxed knowing that even more challenging classes were ahead.

Back at PSU in January and after a very ritualistic great induction into Brotherhood I found out from Joe A in Pre-Med that he had pursued a newly instituted program by three medical schools to take five to six students after three years of undergraduate work of course criteria met. He applied (and was later accepted – the first from PSU) and suggested I consider this. Boy did I! It would save me a year and money. The med schools were Northwestern in Chicago, Temple and Hahnemann in Philadelphia. So, I started the process which, by the way, the Dean of the College of Science did not like the plan. That made getting the proper courses lined up harder but there was no stopping this warrior coal cracker.

Thus, my last two quarters at PSU were busy ones adjusting my courses, getting help where needed (thanks Tom W!), applying to med schools and enjoying off time when I could. In the summer '65 I did get a better job at JM as Ronnie said I would. I worked in the chemical compound quality control lab doing tests so that everything met specification. The summer activities went as the last except less nightlife and more making sure things were ready for the fall.

I returned to PSU for fall quarter, one that I really needed to get a great GPA to aid my early entrance to either Northwestern or Hahnemann in Philadelphia. Temple was eliminated as they had a 21-age rule when entering and I missed that by about four months. So, I really hit the books hard taking just Saturday night for a wild party approach. There were still five football games and intramurals but that was always not a problem.

I did get great grades thanks to tutoring in advanced physics by Tom W., my high school friend and Brother, and friend to this day.

Tom was so intelligent that he would have this strange look on his face when I could not get what he easily understood. Sometimes I was convinced he was an alien having fun on Earth. He graduated 2nd in the class of 1966 in Engineering, did graduate work at MIT and obtained a PhD from NYU. He became a partner with McKenzie Corporation and retired just after 55. He serves on corporation boards, mentors students at Penn State and has given much to the University. Presently he lives on Kiawah Island, SC and travels in Europe in the summer from his base in Copenhagen. Christmas was a welcome break after a real downer of a visit to Washington to get the "new boyfriend, possible engagement" news from AP. I walked away with my head up for a long, foggy bus ride home. Unknown to me the future held more of AP!

In late January of 1966, I was rejected by Northwestern but accepted by Hahnemann! Thus, I had accomplished something I actually early on thought was a pipe dream. Two guys from the same fraternity in two years!

Obviously, I now took my foot off the academic pedal but not to applause from the house as my contribution to the academic contest would be lost. I finally enjoyed the surrounding mountains, campus events, sleeping late and lounging around listening to the Mama and Papa's while never missing a party.

Before parting from South Allen Street, I offer some other great memories:

1. I won a case of good whiskey for providing evidence (two pictures) of a sexual encounter in our frat housemothers home with AP (with her permission of course) – a first! I shared the whiskey with my pledge brothers.

2. We lost the opening football game of 1965 to Michigan State who went on to win the National Championship. They were good, big and nasty!

3. A few hitchhiking trips home. Easy in those days and now unheard of!

4. Walking daily up to 1.5 miles to classes or the library on the far side of campus.

5. An early, weird, May snowstorm in 1964 which forced us out of second story windows in snowshoes to shovel and closed the University for the first time.

6. Meeting many different women from many different places but never finding one that I thought I could possibly spend a lifetime with.

7. The fact that three of us (I, Frank z. and Tom W.) from the same small high school graduating class ended up fraternity brothers at a large university.

8. Women were not allowed in the House unless our House Mother was present. I got fined once for having tea with a woman in the kitchen - $5.00 for conduct unbecoming of a Phi Sig.

9. The overall great experience of a Fraternity – a bunch of guys from all over forming a band of brothers to help each other, have fun together, and excel at academics and sports within a system which has gone with the wind.

So after about five weeks of the summer of 1966 at home to relax and prepare for medical school it was off at the end of June for a new adventure in the "city of brotherly love".

Medical School 1966 – June 1970

A week before starting at Hahnemann, just after July 4th holiday, I got to Philadelphia where my frat brother, Joe A. – now a Sophomore, had set me up with a couple who rented rooms out on Summer Street just a block from Med school. It was a nice three-story row home and they had two rooms each on the second and third floors. I got the smallest room on the third floor with a shared bathroom for $7.00 a week. It had a single bed, a small desk, one small window, minimal closet space, one small fridge and an area suitable for piling books.

I spent the first two years there with only one rent increase to $8.00 per week. And no problems. Before the start of my third year Bruce H. in his last year had an opening in his neat, small townhouse on Historic Mole Street just a couple of blocks away. And it is still there! An older woman who we never met owned it and only charged us $85.00 a month plus electricity which was minimal.

With housing costs low and food manageable (and free on many occasions) financing Med school was not hard with my parents helping a little, a job in the lab for two years, Navy money one summer (later explained) and about $6,000 borrowed I became an M.D. Today people are graduating Medical school with up to $250,000 of debt!

My class of about 120 consisted of five of us taken after three years and only five women. The number of women now is at least 50%. I believe we only had three people drop out deciding a life in medicine was not for them. The first two years were mostly classroom and lab work – physiology, human chemistry, pharmacology, etc. and the best, human anatomy. We had four people to a cadaver for complete dissection learning every aspect of the body. Our cadaver was a scholarly male, age 60, with a neat short beard. We named him The Prophet and treated him with respect.

The coursework was difficult and required long hours and sometimes problems arose with how things were being taught or not. For reasons I cannot recall, I was elected Class President, so I represented us with any problems thus getting to know the Dean and the faculty very well. I remember all issues getting resolved.

The last two years consisted of six-week rotations on all aspects of medicine and surgery. They were at three institutions; Hahnemann Hospital, Philadelphia General and St. Agnes in South Philadelphia for community surgery. There were good and bad aspects of all three with details of life later.

I had about two months "off" in the summer after year one and year two so will detail that here with background.

In 1966, we all faced the prospect of being drafted into the military in the midst of the escalating Vietnam War. At a classmate's suggestion I looked into the Berry Plan with the U.S. Navy. Basically, you joined the Naval Reserve as an Officer (Ensign) with your active duty requirement of at least two years deferred until you finished all residency specialty training. In addition, was the opportunity for money if needed. In return for an additional year or more of duty. Since no one ever dreamed that the draft would be rescinded I thought that this was a sound choice. Thus, sometime in early 1967 I applied, was accepted, passed the physical and mental exams and was sworn in as an Ensign in the U.S. Naval Reserve.

In the "summer" of 1967 I spent two plus months on active duty having found a surgeon Dr. Bill A. doing some interesting research at Bethesda Naval Hospital in Washington D.C. So off I went via train to my housing at the BOQ (Bachelor Officers Quarters) at Bethesda after securing all necessary uniforms. Dr. A. was a great guy and the research was in rats using freeze dried skin for use in burn patients. I learned much from him and it helped me later during my residency in the large burn unit in Richmond, Virginia. The BOQ was great where we had a party every Friday with $1.00 steaks and $.25 drinks well attended by all Officers including of course the nurses who were quite hospitable.

I met a lot of interesting people, took in all of historical D.C. and nearby Civil War battlefields at Bull Run and Antietam. I had two lovely romantic liaisons one with a civilian plastic surgeon and one with a lovely secretary who worked at the Pentagon. They were both memorable and I kept in touch with the surgeon for a while after I left. The secretary pronounced me a "summer fling" and thanked me.

I got in trouble with a 19-year-old irresistible redhead I met at a party in Georgetown. She invited me one weekend to her parent's house on the water near Annapolis. I made two mistakes. I did not ask enough questions and went right there still in my uniform as she picked me up from work. Got there, no parents, should have left as I had a funny feeling about something. But my brain was not working but another part of my anatomy was. Great time, incredible, sensual and interesting girl. Never noticed the neighbors except to say hello when we arrived.

First thing Monday morning Dr. A. called me into his office, said that Captain so and so in the command office wanted to see me immediately in his office and he did not sound cordial. On my way up to the top floor of the tower I realized that the redhead and the captain had the same last name.

I confess that because of stark terror I do not recall all of the one-way conversation with her father, but I distinctly remember hearing, "never see her again" and something about "career ending" and vaguely the word "disappearance". I only said, I believe, "Yes, Sir, sorry." I saluted and left. Dr. A. told me I appeared half way to hell and assumed it was personal, told me to take the day off, the rats will be there tomorrow. After a long run and a few stiff drinks at the bar I slept and became a priest for my last two weeks and never forgot how stupidity, a name on a uniform, and a neighbor taught me a lesson.

The class year of '67-'68 flew by – classes were hard but manageable. The summer of '68 consisted only of June so I spent time at home in Frackville to visit with my parents and friends that made it home. It was a nice month of down time before the clinical years started July 1 of 1968 culminating about two years later with graduation in June 1970. My parents and my brother made it to graduation. My sister had completed her education degree two years previously and was teaching in international schools, so she was abroad in the Dominican Republic at the time.

I saved Philadelphia, sports and social tales of Med school years for last so here goes. And one surprise!

Philadelphia has always been known as the City of Brotherly Love but while I was there for four years I encountered many examples of "screw your brother". And when I arrived one of my classmates who grew up in "Philly" advised me that at 1 A.M. there were two kinds of people on the streets – The Quick and the Dead. I remembered that, and it helped me on a few occasions. I actually liked the city because of all the history in it and nearby.

Near Hahnemann we had a great running route – up the Ben Franklin Parkway and ending going up all the steps of the art museum (just like in the movie Rocky). Places to eat on budget were Dewey's Hot Dogs & Burgers on Broad Street and the Walnut Street Cafeteria a few blocks away, a couple pizza joints and our favorite watering hole the Logan Square Inn. I would be amiss if I neglected my favorite eating places as it came free and with some lovely nurses. That was dinners at the homes or apartments of the many Italian nurses at St. Agnes Hospital when we did our six-week rotations. Loved St. Agnes!

While on eating places, I have one story about Dewey's. They had a '60's juke box and one early evening when four of us were there Mike, one of my classmates, went over and slipped a quarter in the box and a little soft shoe. One of a few African American guys tossed a quarter at his feet and yelled, "Dance white boy, dance". Needless to say, a bit of a fight ensued, cops arrived. Fortunately, no one was hurt and after a lot of talking we were all let go.

I think the police thought the whole thing was amusing and since no harm was done to Dewey's or to any of us combatants it was called another evening in Philly.

The social scene for me in Philadelphia was limited due to the heavy work load, working and occasionally taking the train home to visit my parents. Because of the lack of play money, socializing was limited to mainly house parties and neighborhood bars. One of the really enjoyable once a month encounters took place in my second year when a classmate and a bit older (26 or so) nursing student got a group together to play strip poker. The guys had no rules of engagement, but the women stopped at keeping their panties on. We had a lot of fun, probably a little cheating, but no (at least not at the venue) actual sexual interaction.

I just remember some very nice ladies and some great times with two instances in which I could have lost my life or sustained injury; 1. When after seeing a wonderful secretary on our third date she confessed to me that she was tempted to sleep with me but decided to stay true to her girlfriend! Wow, so I thanked her for her truthfulness and left at 1 A.M. with my umbrella on a rainy night. Midway home I noticed two guys coming up quickly behind me on a quiet street – my analysis was how to avoid a mugging and surprise came to mind. As they got near, I whipped around swatting one in the face with my umbrella and stabbing the other guy in the gut, leaving the umbrella and running like the devil. I never heard anything about the incident, and I had never called the police. All I know is I survived the "streets of Philadelphia". 2. Third year on clinical rotation at Hahnemann I met a cute blonde nurse from Texas. We hit it off having a beer at the Logan Square a couple of times after work. She invited me to dinner at her place on the main line so one Saturday when we were both off, I took wine on the train with the station being close to her apartment on the second floor of three. We were having a nice dinner and I was hoping for a great later encounter when there a was a loud knock on the door. Then arguing and, "I'll kill the son of a bitch" at which I realized that I was the one who fit that bill. Out the window I went dropping into some deep grass hurting my ankle a bit and then off to the train station hearing five or six shots in my direction. Luckily a train arrived quickly and again I made it back alive. The next day she informed me that it was her estranged husband who came to try to take her back to Texas. She was profoundly sorry, but I decided that I had learned a lesson and made my exit. It would have been sad had someone had to send a notification to my parents that sounded like "we regret to inform you your son died because he was…stupid".

My two Logan Square bar encounters – 1. One evening with a nice crowd, three guys with shotguns and masks came in the locked doors and proceeded to take all the money the band had while we were hands up. Interestingly, they left us with our money and drink from the bar. I think it was an inside job – slick and quick and, as I remember, never solved. 2. Another time two of us arrived after rugby for beers at the bar when Dennis saw a guy trying to break into my townhome next to the bar. He told me to call the police and he grabbed a two by four from some building materials in the parking lot. When I came out of the bar after calling, I saw him beating this guy as he tried to get over the fence enclosing the row of houses. The police arrived and watched this while laughing for a minute or two before I let them into the house and out back to arrest the guy. They did not charge Dennis with anything and thanked him for his help even though the intruder kept yelling we were trying to kill him. Another evening in the streets of Philadelphia.

My two rotations at Philadelphia General – 1. One in psychiatry and one in surgery. What a zoo! Saw a lot of trauma and different problems on surgical rotation and learned to mix IV's and take basic X-rays because of short staffing. I learned many skills and was exhausted each day.

On a three-week psych rotation, I saw sad, tormented people of all sorts who were extremely difficult to treat. I remembered one experience our group had with a 30-year-old male who, when asked why he was in the hospital, replied, "I cut off my dick". No one knew what to say and I knew I could never deal with this stuff.

In the sports world during my first year I was introduced to rugby by Pat R., an upperclassman, who played for Philadelphia Rugby Football Club (PRFC). After playing football it sounded, perhaps, more interesting and more difficult and it certainly turned out that way. Thus, I initially started with PRFC practicing and learning in the Spring of 1967.

In the fall we recruited and established the Hahnemann RFC (Rugby Football Club) from the whole medical school community and played our first match in early Spring of 1968. I remember that it was cold with melted snow puddles on the field. We had a good four seasons after that (Fall and Spring) playing other medical schools (Temple & Jefferson) and colleges such as University of Pennsylvania and Lehigh. In Spring of 1969 we won a six-team medical school tournament held in Philadelphia's Fairmount Park and held a great party afterwards.

I remember that party held on Mole Street and the adjacent Logan Square Tavern as a very embarrassing thing happened. I was talking to a really interesting attractive female grad student from

Bryn Mawr College just outside of our townhouse. It was a beautiful day when she suddenly said that it was raining. But as I looked up one of my teammates was urinating out of the window! After a few screams the woman ran away ending a perfectly good conversation. That teammate ended up being a well-respected Professor of Medicine in Boston. Today I wonder if he would have ever made it to professor if this incident, for whatever reason, made it to CNN.

There were three excursions of six weeks each during my clinical years that were unique. In early Spring of 1969, I met a visiting British woman Linda B. She was strikingly beautiful. We hit it off and after she visited a few other places on the East Coast she spent a couple days with me in Philadelphia and invited me to come to London if I could arrange a clinical rotation at one of the hospitals. I got permission from Hahnemann and arranged a six-week rotation at St. George's Hospital in London at Hyde Park Corner. I was excited!

However, only a few days before I was to leave Linda informed me that she was reunited with a boyfriend I never knew she had but had a friend make arrangements with a young family in South London for quarters. Okay, so I did as I have always with a woman who walks away. I turn and I walk through an exit door, looking only at the positive.

So, off to London in early June, met by her friend who was extremely nice, got settled with a nice young family with one child and the next day went right to work at St. George's – a neat double decker bus ride away through Central London.

I learned an awful lot in the English system in regard to history taking a physical diagnosis. Great professors, early days ending at 5 P.M. with earlier afternoon tea. Nice group of classmates who were about six months ahead of me in clinical terms. We made a pact to avoid politics as the Vietnam War was ramping up and the Brits were not happy. While I was there, there were significant riots in the Hyde Park area and near the American Embassy. All were handled well by the police with the restrained use of mounted cavalry in a civilized manner.

I crammed a lot into six weeks:

1. Linda called once and said her parents in the East of England wanted me to visit. I replied yes as long as she was not present. I took a pleasant train ride to the small town where I spent a delightful two days with Mr. and Mrs. B. Took I the historic areas and spent time at the most delightful pub with interesting characters. Linda's parents were lovely people. We did not address her situation.

2. The young couple I stayed with had a brother who was an Air Controller at Dublin airport. They insisted I go for a long weekend to see a part of Ireland and stay with the couple there. Good choice and cheap. The city and history was great and the people very friendly. One of the two nights I had a note with the address of my stay pinned inside my light coat and went off. Ran into two lovely Irish women and a rugby player and what a night we had. A nice cabbie got me home almost at daylight after visiting a pub where cabbies hung out. The note was intact and served its purpose. Then back across the Irish Sea to London and work.

3. I had a few nice evenings with Linda's friend Elaine and an Australian woman I met who devoured jellied eels (an intact eel wrapped around jelly).

4. I took in as much history as possible, made it out to the Royal Enclosure at the Henley Regatta on the Thames River where

I sat next to an English Princess and her grandfather. It would have been nice to be a prince.

5. A visit to a pub with three floors of gay women and men, a ride in an Aston Martin on the M1 roadway doing 140 mph, sneaking into the playboy club for about 40 minutes and riding the Tube (Subway) system. I always picked up a copy of the International Tribune from New York and one time reading on the Tube a guy suddenly bit through the paper! As I said, "What the hell was that for?" he spit out the paper and screamed that I shouldn't care what he did when American soldiers are killing kids in Vietnam. He then ran away, and I sat there wondering what just happened.

I enjoyed the total experience with fond memories. St. George's Hospital closed years ago but the entrance façade was left up for historical reasons. It is now the entrance to the most expensive hotel in London. I thanked all my British friends and mentors and flew west across the pond to complete my last year at Hahnemann.

Late summer began my search for a surgical residency as I decided that was going to be my life. I loved the challenge, the excitement and the awards of solving a problem or saving a life. Being in the operating room in charge of a team to make someone's life better was the ultimate experience. Better than a Marine in a firefight having to end a life! After a lot of research and thought I narrowed my choices down to the Medical College of Virginia in Richmond, Jefferson in Philadelphia and Hahnemann for insurance. I was also interested in Ohio State as my rugby mate Dennis K. was there and encouraged me to check it out. So, in early fall I got permission to do a month on the Chief of Surgery, Dr. Z's rotation.

Off to Columbus where I stayed at my fraternity and also played rugby with the Ohio State Club. It was a busy month to say the least. Dr. Z. had everything done his way and ran a very tight service, demanding and giving no quarter. However, after an incident in the O.R. with our chief resident Dr. Gary R. I decided probably not. During a difficult stomach operation which Dr. R. was doing, Dr. Z helping along with me, the spleen was injured beyond repair and had to be removed. Dr. Z. was furious. He took the gloved hand of Gary and put a clamp on the skin on his hand, told him to get out and don't take the clamp off until he was out of sight. I was mildly horrified as I watched this, and Dr. Z. and I finished without a word about Gary.

I later asked Gary about it and he said it was part of the job of working for a great surgeon such as Dr. Z. and he would be okay. I came to the conclusion that working under a different fine surgeon without the possibility of personal physical agony would be a better choice. Dr. Z. really wanted me and even called me twice. I did say that I would not withdraw my application because of the difficulty of getting a good position but hoped for Richmond which, I found out in early winter, I did get.

Finally, I get to the surprise in my life which had twists and turns I never saw coming. In the early Spring of 1969 at a house party I met S.D. She was tall with long light brown hair, striking eyes and a wonderful slightly mischievous smile – an Irish beauty born of parents who immigrated just before WWII broke out. She was a nurse and a year older than me. I was, I admit, intrigued more so than with anyone since A.P. We saw each other a few times before I left for England and that intensified upon my return. There seemed to be something special about her. And unlike other women intimacy ended short of sexual intercourse.

I was, I believe, falling in love with S.D. and considered marriage. I did purchase an engagement ring which I planned to hold for a while until I was sure of the future. I really loved rugby and continued on playing as will be detailed to some degree. My only initial injury was a bent left pinky finger which never bothered me as a surgeon and could have provided an ID had I lost my head somewhere!

Around March of 1970 I received word that I had matched with the Medical College of Virginia and would be an intern starting July 1. S.D. and I decided to give it a go together in Richmond and so plans moved ahead. She secured a job in the clinical research department and we secured and apartment in Henrico County just outside of Richmond.

I knew I was going to a good program with lots of operating experience, but I had some anxiety about being a Yankee in the Capital of the Confederacy. I knew that there were deep feelings yet about the Civil War as most of Richmond was burned by the Army of the Potomac. However, I was excited by all the history and opportunity for exploring as much as I could over five years.

So, after graduation from Hahnemann and a short vacation we set off in one car towing a U-Haul on Route 95 to Richmond. And the beat goes on.

Internship and General Surgical Residency – Richmond Virginia - July 1970 – July 1975

We arrived at "home" outside of Richmond a week before the hammer hit the road July 1 of 1970. Enough time to get the apartment settled, plan the logistics of getting to work and of daily living and realizing that this was not Philadelphia.

The Civil Rights (Act) bill was passed just five years earlier and it was evident that implication was just slowly moving along and things we enjoyed in the city were just evolving and very slowly. MCV had two hospitals – one for blacks and the other for everyone else, now it was a Women's Hospital and General Hospital, Medical ER and Surgical ER. You had to bring your own alcohol and wine to a restaurant and most everything was closed on Sunday. Country Clubs, as I remember, were White Anglo-Saxon men only and interracial marriages were unknown. One social issue I discovered and was surprised by was the sexual promiscuity in the medical community – "Sleepy Richmond" was really awake at all hours at MCV.

On July 1 we were right out of the block and it was obvious this was going to be hard and demanding training with a workload of every other night on call most the time. My first rotation as an intern was on Orthopedics and I was given maximum responsibility for patient care. Trauma was a good 50% of our work. Other rotations were General Surgery, Vascular, Neuro Surgery, OB-GYN, Urology and the burn unit as an intern.

Then the next four years of residency were General and Vascular Surgery, Transplant and Burn unit and Pediatric Surgery with rotations on head and neck Oncology at the VA Hospital. Cardiothoracic was available years three and four.

Dr. D.H. was our Chief, a brilliant transplant surgeon, the kind of man you would follow anywhere. His loyal second Dr. H.M.L. was a terrific teacher as was our head Pediatric Surgeon Dr. A.S. – whose trademark "Swank (or anyone else) you are slow but poor". Our head burn surgeon Dr. B.W.H. was your consummate southern gentleman and a fine precise surgeon. We were on the cutting edge of Neurosurgery with a brilliant young surgeon and Cardiothoracic surgery was making great strides with Dr. R.L.

On a history note, Dr. H.M. was the grandson of the Confederate surgeon who amputated the left arm of General "Stonewall" Jackson. All of these men and many other people provided me with the ability to make excellent decisions both in and out of the operating room in an exciting but deliberate environment. We were expected to work hard and long, and we did without complaint. The number of hours we spent in the hospital would not be allowed in the training programs of today. But we were ready to practice without more supervision right out of the box, something in most cases we do not see today.

Rather than try to remember events year by year in such an intense training environment I will give you stories and events which were interesting, colorful and eye opening.

On a personal side, SD and I decided to start a marriage and did so with a relatively small ceremony over a few days off over Christmas 1970 in Northern Philadelphia. We went about our lives until things changed a lot in the Spring of 1972. On background there was during this time a lot of political tension between MCW and Virginia Commonwealth University over many issues and we were caught in the web. The issue was a parking space. When SD came to work in the morning and I was working the ER until 8 A.M. she notified me where the car was parked, and I would pick it up. The VCU police who patrolled the whole MCV-VCU campus area were very strict on parking.

One morning as I was arriving to get the car in a small lot next to the Research Center where SD worked, I came on a scene with two police cars and a large policeman pulling SD out of the car with her obviously frightened and screaming. I tried to stay calm and intervened only to try to help. I was arrested as was SD and we were both placed in a paddy wagon and taken to the Richmond jail. So began a fight that started over a simple parking issue and a scared 26-year-old nurse.

We obtained a competent lawyer with the help of Dr. H. and began our quest for freedom. SD was charged with resisting arrest. The Richmond DA would ask for two years in jail for each of us!

I learned two things that I still believe during the ensuing process: 1. You are assumed guilty and not the other way around as the law states. That is bullshit. You must prove your innocence. 2. Use every tactic that you can to win – within the law and skirting it. Give no quarter.

We discovered much about this officer including the fact that he had beat up his own father and threw him out of their home just weeks before the incident. Also came to light the political nonsense including how the President of VCU wanted to see us in jail to make a point. It truly felt like a battle in the Civil War.

Fortunately, the jury trial came quickly. The judge was a bit harsh in not allowing some of the issues with the officer as evidence, but our lawyer was up to the task, was clever and relentless. We were found not guilty of the charges much to our relief. So ended the ordeal of two Yankees in a southern court but it took a toll on SD. As for me I continued work as usual and never sat as a juror at trial because of my belief that when charged you are guilty.

Over the next one and a half years SD slipped into a state of anxiety and at times depression which led to alcohol abuse. We had bought a small townhome in the up and coming fan district of Richmond which did not help in her case. I did not recognize the true depth of her problem until near the end of my residency in Richmond.

After consultation with her sister and the realization that SD and I could not continue together she was placed in alcohol rehabilitation in Philadelphia. All this was complicated by the fact that I had developed an intimate relationship with a nurse in the hospital during all this turmoil.

Thus, ended a relationship which probably needed a calmer, less stressful environment to be successful. Looking back, I should have put any relationship on hold knowing the years in Richmond were going to be filled with long days and nights of work. SD did recover, remained sober, and had a successful career eventually in administrative nursing. And to my knowledge she has had a long-term relationship later in life. We occasionally correspond.

Outside of this major problem there were hard mundane times, good times and sad times which I will tell you about.

1. I loved the history available within 90 miles of Richmond and when I had time, took maximal advantage of especially the Civil War battlefields and Williamsburg.

2. Sexual promiscuity was rampant in that everyone seems to be looking for some variety. Also, we had sleeping quarters across the street from the hospital leading to access for affairs and each Friday we had "liver rounds" (a party in the cafeteria for anyone not working) which led to liaisons until put to rest when a group of wives found out. We had one tragedy: one of my fellow residents was discovered in bed with a nurse in the quarters by his wife. She shot him but not the nurse. He survived, and his wife went to jail for attempted murder. That toned things down.

   I must confess that I did partake of the availability of women for sexual adventures and/or simple interludes. That included a beautiful African-American secretary daughter of a prominent Richmond preacher and in my last year a very striking, tall, all legs nurse I will remember always.

3. A prime example of hard work was a severe nursing shortage which lasted over two months. Dr. H. called us all together and informed us of required double duty. We took nursing shifts along with our training. I believe that during that time I went home perhaps four times. But I learned a deep appreciation for the roll of nurses and carried that forward. This obviously would never happen today, but we did not even think of not helping. We just did it. Another example of will over the body is when in my second residency year while on the burn service I developed acute appendicitis. Dr. H.M.L. removed my appendix on a Saturday evening around 6 PM.

Because there was only one other resident to cover, I simply sucked it up and was back on the burn unit Monday morning.

4. The VA Hospital was an experience in compassion because of the head and neck cancer service. Long delicate, disfiguring operations along with dealing with the recurrent disease was a lesson in life. When patients came in with recurrences of cancer with no good solution and slowly bleeding from exposed blood vessels, we offered simple humane care which was almost always accepted. Medication was given to let them go to eternal sleep. I am not sure how this would be conducted in today's environment but then it was the ultimate compassionate care as I saw it. Lighter sides of the VA were dealing with cockroaches in the sleeping quarters. One jumped on me while shaving one morning but after a five-minute battle, I won! We had good times talking with patients about experience in the service, had good get-togethers with the staff after work and had the opportunity for evening breaks when we had some excess coverage. Smoking on the wards was allowed back then and one day while on burn duty at MCV a patient arrived from the VA with a note by the resident saying, "patient found still smoldering in bed"! Fortunately, the burns were not severe, and he survived.

5. We did get some vacation time which I spent visiting my parents, exploring historic places and roaming the then still sleepy areas of the outer banks of North Carolina in the summer. I grew my beard there in the Summer of 1974 and never have been without it since. I also continued to play rugby as much as possible first with the VCU team and then with James River RFC. These were all good times with good down-home people and some good rugby. During summers

a surgical device rep always had a pig roast. I remember one where a fellow resident T.G. and I ate brains with Tabasco sauce right out of the skull (after a few beers). Dr. H. also had a picnic every summer at his farm away from Richmond – always a great time. Dr. S. never attended as he said, "It's a long way to go for a hot dog.".

6. More happenings: I learned never to talk a patient into surgery. T.G., a resident above me, did this with a 70-year-old lady with an intraabdominal mass. She finally said, "ok sonny you can operate but I am going to die". He reassured her very much. In surgery the next day she had a cardiac arrest just as T.G. was ready to open her up. She did not survive, and we were all in disbelief but at least I learned a lesson.

On Christmas Eve as a first-year resident we admitted a large African American woman named R.W. with acute Cholecystitis (gall bladder). We hoped she would cool down and we could then operate in two or three days. No luck. We went into the O.R. around 5 PM with minimal staff as everyone fled if possible. I was in the room by myself with her when she began screaming, "I'm falling." She was flailing on the table and ready to tumble off when I went to my knees and looked up in time to stabilize this very large butt coming at me while yelling for help. I was saved from embarrassment at best and suffocation at worst. The Richmond paper would have had a field day with this story!

Dr. H. for a while got onto this bandwagon of treating morbid obesity with a small bowel bypass procedure which initially was successful but later too many complications involving liver dysfunction put the procedure to rest. But not before we had our share of stories. We became a "center" for this and so had people from all over the East come to Richmond. A woman from New Jersey who couldn't stand being on the required five-day liquid diet prior to operation actually successfully had a full dressed turkey delivered to her in the lobby from the Jefferson hotel. The nurses called us early in the morning prior to the scheduled operation and we found her grinning ear to ear pleased that she devoured most of the turkey. The second degree burn on her abdomen where she hid the turkey under her bath robe did not phase her!

The largest person we had a Mr. G.S., age 35 or so, who arrived from North Carolina in the back of a pickup truck. We had to weigh him on the docks on the James River and he came in at around 830 lbs. Patients were put in the clinical research center where the very next day G.S. caused a frantic call to be placed to us. On arrival we found him wedged in a bathroom on a crushed commode with water flowing all around. The fire department guys had to knock out a section of wall to retrieve him. From then on he urinated and had bowel movements in a tub, was put on a diet, lost 200 lbs. and then we operated on him. He survived to our surprise and actually went back to North Carolina but unfortunately was lost to follow up.

I helped Dr. H. operate on A.H. perhaps the most famous trumpet player in New Orleans and before he left, he treated us to a small concert which included some beautiful women. He lost weight but later had the operation reversed because of the liver complications. We were all glad when this type of operation was put to rest. We had enough to deal with.

7. The surgical emergency room was a complete zoo full of almost everything that could happen to an individual. When I took my turns being in charge I knew that we had the ability to take care of whatever came through the door. We worked hard and saved many lives including those who took the life of another. I never enjoyed this part of my training that involved the repairing of what people did to each other. I am not sure that anyone did.

   The worst we saw was a Saturday night when a motorcycle group from Washington D.C. attacked a gathering of the Confederate Angels Motorcycle group in North Richmond. The carnage was awful. Our trauma teams operated on nine people and we pronounced about eight dead in the E.R. All of the nine survived. Thank God we only saw this much horror only once, but many other days gave us one or two.

   The most amusing sight I saw was conducted by our head nurse, Mrs. L. on a very busy early evening. A man ran into the E.R., stopped right in the middle of our main area and screamed that snakes were all over him and do something. I looked at Mrs. L. who quickly ran to a closet and returned with a broom. She told him to stand still and proceeded to brush him with the broom and swept the "snakes" away. The man smiled, thanked her and ran out. Great work by Mrs. L.

8. The best advice I received while at MCV came when I was an intern. It was from the Chief Resident Dr. G.W. wo pulled me aside and said, "Swank, I hear you are a great intern." "Always remember that the only good way to take care of your patients is to first assume that everyone else is out to kill

them." That stuck with me and made me aware of the whole atmosphere of patient care.

Another fond memory of hard work and the dedication at MCV was Dr. S.St. P. ahead of me two years who in 1956 fought the Russians in the Hungarian Revolution in Budapest as a 15-year-old. We had a resident join us from Boston who was a good looking South African Caucasian playboy type who like to operate but not work hard. S.P. was a workhorse 6'5", 250 lbs. One day as we were on late day rounds S.P., because of something Dr. P.M. said about going home, grabbed him and put him up against a wall and said, "I killed a Russian with my bare hands and if you don't wise up and work, I'll kill you." Needless to say, we had no further problems with Dr. P.M.!

Lastly, thoughts on a tragedy, a change, a decision and an end to life in Richmond –

Dr. Hume was a man of many talents and interests one of which was being a pilot. He loved it but none of us who had any knowledge of his flying especially Dr. HML, were always concerned about his concentration in the air. In fact, I know that Dr. H.M.L. on more than on occasion said directly to Dr. H. – David, please don't fly anymore."

On May 21, 1973, at age 55, Dr. H. died instantly when his plane crashed into the side of a mountain in Southern California. When the news reached Richmond, it was like a complete shock wave of sorrow came over everything. I remember thinking of the lyrics from Dr. H's favorite song, "Bye bye Miss American Pie" by Don McLean. It was the day "the music died".

Dr. B.W.H. assumed leadership of the program until just before my last year starting in July 1974 when Dr. L.G. was hired.

Everything changed. The excitement, high energy, and we can do anything and everything attitude of Dr. H. was gone. Since I was new Chief Resident, I was able to have a frank chat with Dr. G. and conveyed the feelings of the house staff leaving an open door.

As time went by, we could definitely sense a change (as we expected) to a more "tight ship" approach, more formality and less fun. We endured and for me it was 10-11 months until I left Richmond. I had narrowed down my career choices to Neurosurgery, Orthopedics and Cardiothoracic surgery ultimately deciding on CT surgery as it was an exciting, evolving field. I began to look at programs as the slot at MCV with Dr. R.L. was already promised to one of my fellow residents.

I interviewed at Stanford, Moffit in San Francisco, Medical College of Wisconsin in Milwaukee and Texas Heart Hospital. I planned at that stage in my career to stay in academic medicine, so a year of research would be beneficial. After all was researched and visited, I ended up signing with the program in Milwaukee as it offered the year of research to begin, thereby, giving me a bit of a break after five tough years. The most interesting part of the whole process was a social night with the residents in San Francisco late Fall of 1974. They took me to a club in the city which had live sex acts on stage, no movies! I had never seen anything like that or since. What a strange world!

So, by May of 1975 it was settled that Milwaukee was the next step. I did this knowing that the Chief there was leaving and an interim Chief whom I met was now in place. Since nothing else changed, I decided to go, putting aside a last-minute visit to the University of Michigan. As you will see, maybe I should have made that flight.

A last social surprise occurred at MCV when Dr. A.S., Chief of Pediatric Surgery, married an African American woman. I still felt Richmond culture shaking like an earthquake when I hit the road for a stop in Pennsylvania before driving forever in Ohio and Indiana to Milwaukee and another adventure in another place.

July 1975 to July 1978 – Milwaukee, Wisconsin

I drove to Milwaukee in my older model used car having earlier secured a townhouse apartment around a small lake in the north part of the city. Shipped a few essential pieces of furniture as most sold with the home in Richmond. I sent S.D. half the money from the sale to help her with her recovery.

I settled into the lab at County Hospital conducting research already underway on myocardial preservation. Dr. D.L. who hired me has a project going with a Dr. S. so I jumped right in. Dr. B.L. the head pediatric cardiac surgeon was interim chief while a search committee did their job.

It was nice to have a break from the grind of MCV and so I got back into rugby with the Milwaukee Club and later joined the newly formed Westside Harlequins where I played two of my three years. My only injury was a broken right foot early in the fall which cost me the fall season playing but not the parties. The slower time also allowed me to visit my parents a couple of times along with my sister and my brother both teaching back east. I also visited tall, lovely B. in Richmond who informed me that she was coming to Milwaukee to work at the VA hospital and live with an old girlfriend. That happened quickly and led to many wonderful intimate afternoons and evenings. Between B. and rugby, I only had enough left in me for research.

That became complicated when another Nurse B decided to come to Milwaukee before a job would open up in California. I agreed to take her and her cat in for a while until she could find something. She turned out to be sexually kinky and had me every which way but loose! This turned out to be a longer stay and another cat brought in which turned out to be pregnant. That cat, for whatever reason, liked me. On New Year's Eve, after returning from a party with B., I was sleeping soundly after a round of her sexual needs. I awoke with a wet back and quickly discovered about six newborn kittens romping on me! The cat had used me for an initial home. From then on it was pussies galore all over and things went downhill.

After about six weeks, I came home to find a note from B. She made a list of eight demands in order for her to stay; the first two were to stop playing rugby and shave off my beard. I do not remember the other six as I stopped after two and started packing her stuff and cats. The next day I found her an apartment for her to figure out where she would end up.

Meanwhile, as the year of research went on we were informed of a new Head of CT Surgery coming in March of '76. We knew there would be a change but what came next change much for me. When Dr. LB arrived, he set out to revamp the program slowly but surely. This affected me directly and set unexpected plans in motion.

Dr. B. called me into his office soon after his arrival and informed me that I was to wrap up my research project with Dr. S ASAP and start a project of his interest. I had no choice but to comply or leave. Dr. S. was so upset he had a complete breakdown requiring care. It was sad to see. I did, however, get to publish a nice paper and present it at a Society of Thoracic Surgeons meeting the following January. But the turn of events began to give me second thoughts about a career in Academic CT Surgery.

After completing my research year in August of 1976, most of the next year was spent on clinical rotation at Children's Hospital in downtown Milwaukee and St. Luke's Hospital in South Milwaukee. St. Luke's was the prominent Cardiac Center in the state and the amount and quality of work there was excellent as was the teaching. I was comfortable with the whole atmosphere at both hospitals and felt that I did a good job.

Upon my return to County Hospital with Dr. B. in charge I began after a few weeks to feel uncomfortable in a regimented, tense atmosphere that seemed to have been built up. It was the first time in my career that I felt this way and it bothered me. It even extended to social situations with Dr. B. As an example, his about eight-year-old son was interested in seeing a rugby match. So, Dr. B. allowed him to go to one of our matches when I was off, but later dressed me down in a demeaning manner when he found out his son had a hot dog at the match. I do not know if it was related to their Jewish religion. After that it only got worse. Even in the operating room I was more and more uncomfortable and for the first time felt unable to adequately do my job.

We subsequently had a discussion in his office where he informed me that he was not going to let me try to finish the program. I found myself agreeing and was actually relieved. He did say that he would not do anything to make it difficult to pursue another program. I knew that my other mentors did not feel the same as Dr. B. so that, I felt, would help to start off on a new experience somewhere. Any thought of a career in Academics was now dust in the wind. I walked out and said to myself, "Okay, now what?". It was now mid Fall of 1977, so I had to find something by next June if I were to become a qualified Cardiothoracic Surgeon.

The first order of business was finding some job for eight months and a way to reduce expenses and eventually a new car as mine was nearing the end. A rugby friend of mine offered to share his two bedroom, very basic, apartment on the East side and I jumped at that. Even better was that one of the private cardiothoracic groups in Milwaukee whom I had met through meetings, kindly offered me a position in the group to assist with procedures, do some myself and care for patients until I could find a program for completion for training for certification. I had completed my certification in General Surgery by passing the written and oral exams. The group was extremely kind and generous to me during this period of transition.

For a reason I cannot remember, I checked about openings in either of the Naval programs. San Diego and Bethesda. A crack in the heavy curtain of life appeared in that Bethesda had a slot open for July 1 of 1978 for a two-year residency followed by two more years of active duty. This would fulfill my commitment under the Berry plan which I had signed into in 1967. After preliminary paperwork I spent two days in Washington D. C. in early Spring of 1978.

My interview with the Chief of CT Surgery, Captain H.A. was honest and very cordial. He was the kind of person one felt very comfortable with immediately. I was very honest and truthful regarding my leaving the program in Milwaukee because of the difficulties with Dr. B I held nothing back.

Dr. A did his homework having already spoken with several people in Milwaukee including Dr. B. He said that Dr. B did not say anything that would prevent me from succeeding in another program. I was frankly surprised. It was a good visit overall including conversations with other staff and two residents. I returned to Milwaukee to await a decision.

Dr. A called a few days later and told me that he would be pleased to have me at Bethesda. That was a huge relief. I immediately informed Drs. K and J.J., the cardiothoracic surgeons I was working with, and subsequently, thanked the surgeons who supported me at St. Luke's and Dr. L at Children's Hospital. I never spoke to Dr. B. as I felt that he wouldn't give a damn.

I would report three weeks prior July 1, 1978 for active duty, uniforms, orientation and "charm school" (about a week of learning military ways and regulations). Thus, I had to gear up in regard to housing and a new car, go through my belongings and so forth. My sister was working in Washington at the time and kindly volunteered to stay with her until I decided where to live.

I got a bonus from Mayfair Thoracic, the group I worked for and had put together $5,000 plus for a car. I found a nice '78 Oldsmobile Cutlass that was listed for more than I had. After some hard bargaining with the salesman, plus embellishment of serving my county stuff, he yelled as I was walking out the door, "Alright you son of a bitch, I'll sell it to you." ($5,000 + tax!) That car turned out to be so far the best I ever owned. It eventually went along through future family and lasted for about 280,000 miles with good care.

So as June of 1978 arrived, I headed south once again for another adventure. But before we go there, I will revisit the social part of three years in Milwaukee.

My life outside of research, residency and a few months of working revolved mainly around rugby and women. Early on the two D's were a major part of my life in the evening but there were also some other interesting women from various aspects of life and one who became a keeper, at least for a while. More later. The people I met in the rugby world were the salt of the earth and great to be around and always helpful. Plus, there is one thing I learned, that a rugby person is always welcome in any other rugby circle in any part of the world. It is true today. We had great, competitive matches and great times afterwards.

I had with me at all times surgical suture sets and other items for injury needs. One time I sutured three guys on a pool table at a local Irish bar after a match. The owner was upset over a couple drops of blood on the cloth, but we had that cleaned. Fortunately, I did not see any really serious injuries, but they are rare in rugby, especially today with the emphasis on safety.

There were two iconic bars on the East side of town where we met for mingling, excursions and many women – The Up ad Under (a rugby term) and Wolski's which had been open forever or so it seemed. Once, one of these women simply handed me a soft vial and said, "sniff this". I complied, and my head popped for a bit as it was amyl nitrate which dilates all vessels. Last time for that – a little bit of marijuana once in a while was my limit. Once in the summer we had a lady strip to panties on top of the bus before going to a baseball game and then the driver was offered $50 if he made no stops the seven miles or so to the stadium. He did it by every trick and path known.

My initial love interest A. tracked me down and came for a visit to "get reacquainted". She looked great and was now unattached. She still smoked Newport cigarettes, had the same husky sexy voice and had even more sexual stamina. I now knew how to find her when I went to Bethesda.

I met D.W. while at Children's Hospital. She was a really good pediatric nurse who lived nearby on the East side. She was lovely and very fit, one of eight kids (five girls) being raised by their mother as their father had recently died. There was something about her that was good and wholesome in addition to a raw sexiness. We did a lot together and with her siblings whom I got close to. After a while I really settled into a nice relationship to the point of my asking her to think about a possible future together. We agreed that my departure south may end it all, but it may also find a different course.

My last interesting encounter in Milwaukee was unexpected. During my research year there was another resident doing research who had connections all over town with many people. He knew one of the Black Milwaukee Bucks basketball players (professional) named J.P. One day the three of us went to an Italian restaurant on the East side known for some notorious patrons. It was a quiet, late lunch when a 60-ish, well-dressed man with three "mafia types" called over to T. and to bring J.P. The scene appeared amiable to me, but I heard nothing. T. had a short conversation with the man as J.P. and I were going to the car. Later, after dropping off J.P. I asked about what happened in the restaurant. It was explained to me that the man was T's uncle and the head of a Milwaukee crime family.

After the man Mr. T.M. told T. never to bring that "N-----" into the joint again, T. told Mr. T.M. that J.P. was a friend of mine and he was sorry and contrite. I did not go near the place after that but did have several amazing times with a woman who was within the "Family" – got away with it but in retrospect it was stupid but many times my brains were too far south.

So, in a little less than three years I faced a possible career ending situation with some perseverance, timing and luck. I learned that people can affect your life in a negative way in addition to a positive way and one must be smart to know the difference and savvy and tough to survive the negatives.

June 1978 to May 1982 – in the United States Navy

In early June I got situated in my sister's apartment in Arlington across the Potomac River from D.C. and made it through Charm School without incident. Now I was in the "real" Navy with the rank of Lieutenant.

I started at Bethesda Naval Hospital on July 1 ad was pleased with the staff with the exception of one of the two other residents who happened to be a woman. She was regimented, not very friendly and overbearing at times. But I needed to live with what I now had as it was my only choice. The only other hospital we went to was the Washington Children's Hospital with two civilian Pediatric Cardiac surgeons.

The call was split every third night and every third weekend, so it was quite manageable. At Children's it was the same deal. The work of care of patients and operating went smoothly from the start completely free of the anxiety I had in Milwaukee with Dr. B. That was soon forgotten.

Overall it was a pleasant two plus year experience both operating and interaction with everyone at Bethesda. The only situation I encountered that was bothersome on a personal and professional basis was at the Children's Hospital. During my rotation there it became evident to me that one of the surgeons was not performing up to the needed standard of care. This became evident in his judgment and conduct of some procedures.

Initially thinking about my own situation in Milwaukee with Dr. B. I hesitated to say anything to the Chief Surgeon. However, after a case involving obviously bad decisions and subsequent death of the child, I had to talk with our Chief. After a full investigation, the surgeon was forced to resign. I was given credit for bringing the problems to light, but I still had mixed feelings for possibly ruining a career while recharging my own. I do not know what eventually happened to him, but I always hoped he turned things around and was successful.

On the personal side of my life, I did find an apartment closer to Bethesda, thanked my sister and moved with minimal furniture in early Fall. I kept in touch and visited D.W. in Milwaukee with us now contemplating living together as she could easily get a job in the Washington Children's Hospital.

However, with this being on and off there were opportunities for some exciting times for me in our nation's Capital with old and new female interests. I also, at almost 33, was still testosterone driven especially with still playing as much rugby as possible with the Washington Rugby Club.

I spent my off-duty time with A.P. as she was still in Washington and a plastic surgeon whom I met when last in D.C. - good times but nothing serious. I thought about A.P. for a long time and tried to figure out my affinity for her – in the end we both talked and realized we had an intense physical relationship. However, our long-term goals were different and "us" would not work out. I must say that she was the most alluring woman I ever met who had that movie actress appeal and an intensity for living life to the max. I did not feel that I could do my job and keep up with her. She needed a top Indy car driver with lots of money and a need to live fast. I met an interesting woman whose father owned a big shipping company (ocean going) in Baltimore and was a major contributor to the Democratic Party. Thus, she had access to the high social circle including the Kennedy's. She was at the party in New England when Ted Kennedy was involved in the accident with a young woman who died. Interesting observations by her which I will leave to the readers imagination.

Then there was the daughter of a retired officer and his wife from Hilton Head, South Carolina. Dr. A. and I did major aortic surgery on her mother which was very successful. The daughter was the classic example of an incredibly beautiful Southern Belle who invited me to experience her version of gratitude for a job well done. All I can say is that from my humble apartment to a beautiful beach on the South Carolina coast of Hilton Head she treated me to the best "thank you" I ever experienced. She wanted to continue a serious relationship, but she had two other men pursuing her and I needed to just keep my focus on my career. I could never have kept up to the lifestyle she wanted and was used to. We parted peacefully and lovingly.

Just before the start of 1979 into our operating room arrived a woman representing a state-of-the-art electrocautery machine. When she emerged from the dressing room after for a meeting, three of us stood there not believing that this tall, athletic woman with long blonde beautiful hair and fantastic legs was the same woman in the operating room. Now, in only a day and an evening she J.L. became a rival to D.W. for my heart and my mind.

So, for the next year my personal situation revolved around two women with different outlooks on many things. The biggest difference was that D.W. was interested in having a family while J.L. who had one son with a Naval Aviator who then left her was not interested in any more children. This would play a major role as time went on.

In January of 1979, South African friends of D.W. and I from Milwaukee days (the husband played rugby with us) proposed a trip through their country for three weeks with two other Americans. I jumped at the chance as I became interested in British-Zulu history in South Africa after reading a great book entitled *The Washing of the Spears*. It took some work for me to get leave time and permission from the South African government as a Naval officer, but I prevailed. So, by mid-January we were off to Johannesburg from New York on South African Airways having jumped through all visa hoops and rules of the Apartheid (separation of blacks and whites) government.

So, after a long flight which included refueling on a God forsaken island called Isle del Sol off the West African Coast, D.W. and I and our two other Americans were hosted by Hilary and adjusted for two days in Johannesburg before setting off for our great adventure in a large VW van. While in JoBurg, as the white South Africans called it, we went to a native dancing ceremony at a large diamond mine. It was very impressive and interesting and also our first large scale look at Apartheid as blacks and whites were seated separately with whites in the shade. The nest day T. and I were topping off our supplies with some beer for the initial phase of the trip. We pulled up in front of the store with two entrances – one said Europeans, the other Non-Europeans. So, we said "well we are not Europeans" so walked in the left side. We were greeted by a group of black guys who were laughing as we were a sight and said, "hey mon, what you doin' here?" We said we are Americans and here to get some beer. There were howls of laughter but then explanations as we were in the blacks only side! Everyone was good, we got the beer and chalked it up to not realizing what was going on.

So, the five of us set off for Krueger National Park in the Northeast. The park was a once in a lifetime experience with seeing many different animals in the wild including lions, cheetahs, giraffes, springboks and elephants. But the most amazing creature to me was this; while slowly driving on atypical dirt road I was astonished to see a ball of dung (elephant droppings) rolling along at a good clip! We stopped and saw the amazing sight of a large beetle propelling the dung along! H explained that this was a "dung beetle" doing his or her part for the home of the beetles - a true shithouse!! Wow! Nature truly produces oddities.

We next headed South to Natal, home of the Zulus. This had me excited. We stayed with his uncle who had a large citrus ranch and could speak the language well – difficult with many clicking sounds. We visited the British-Zulu battle sites of Ishanlawana and Rorke's Drift on the 100th year anniversary of each. The first was a terrible loss by the British and the latter an incredible successful defense of a missionary station by an Engineering corps and infantry regiment of about 150 men against 5000 Zulu warriors. This was depicted in the famous movie *Zulu* where Michael Caine made his acting debut. Twelve Victoria Crosses, the equivalent of our Medal of Honor was awarded for this engagement – the most ever in British Military history. At Ishanlawana I picked up bullet casings and a uniform button which I have today. At Rorke's Drift, I took pictures and made measurements of the area and years later I constructed a diorama to scale (5 feet to 1 inch) of the battle. Today that sits in my home in South Carolina.

We also visited a remote small village of Zulu cattle farmers. I struck up a conversation with the elder via our kind interpreter and ended up making a neat trade. The elder wanted my Timex watch and my binoculars and in return he gave me an Asagi – a Zulu stabbing spear used by his grandfather. For me it was a treasure find and for him, he loved the glasses as he could more easily follow his cattle in the field!! Interesting world!! I loved Natal and the stark vast Drakensburg mountains.

Our next phase of our journey was a somewhat harrowing ride over a narrow dirt mountain road to a remote resort on the wild Coast of South Africa well Southwest of Durban. For a reason I cannot recall we did the last part of the ride at night with me driving and T. laying on the floor for the van with a lantern and the door open. He watched so we did not come close to a deadly drop and I hugged the side of the mountain. Fortunately, this was a one-way dirt road!

As we neared the Umgazi River for a bridge to get to the coast I felt relief, but it was short lived. We were onto the bridge when H. yelled "stop"! I was able to stop us about 20 feet short of certain death as the bridge was washed out!

We turned around and were parked by the river when we heard "putt, putt, putt" coming by. It was a pontoon boat which we hailed and were able to barter ourselves and our van over the river to the resort. We arrived late but alive, greeted by our English owners and were properly quartered after a few drinks to tone us down.

In the morning we awoke to a beautiful sunrise, spent the day exploring the beach as the mountains joined the beach – a truly wild place and a fine two days of exploration and good conversation with other guests.

We then made our way down the coast visiting his home in Knysna, then made a swing Northwest to the wine region and then down to Cape Town and the Cape of Good Hope. My highlight there was a personal tour of Newlands Rugby Stadium – one of the great world venues and visiting the Cape of Good Hope area. Right at the Southernmost point you can look out and clearly see the mixing of the blue Indian Ocean with the green of the South Atlantic. Amazing and I have a picture to prove it!

It was then time to hand in our rented and trusted VW van, catch a flight to Johannesburg and then back to New York and then Washington D.C. it was an amazing, wonderful and knowledgeable trip – full of incredible sights and sounds and events that made the hair on your neck stand up. D.W. felt the same way and we grew closer.

When back, it was a lot of work over the next few months with only breaks coming with J.L. and D.W. but I began to feel I needed to make a decision.

I did make a trip to Boulder, Colorado to visit J.L. in her home setting. It was a wonderful, sincere time in a beautiful place. We discussed much, loved a lot, and when I left, I still did not know which way to go – with her a life of only ourselves to worry about save for her son or a family life with D.W. – her family plus our future one.

I finally decided that I would like to have a family someday and hoped that J.L. understood. She was very gracious, and we agreed to remain friends and keep in touch. That decision was not easy for me to make and even harder to convey to J.L. D.W. came in April and secured a job at Washington Children's Hospital, I completed my residency in June and for a while stayed on at Bethesda.

In late summer I received word that I would be sent to San Diego Naval Hospital in California as a surgeon was needed to fill a post. My obligated duty would be until June 1982. However, and I will make it short; a senator from South Carolina intervened for another CT surgeon and got him the post in San Diego. I then was slated to fill a need at Portsmouth Naval Hospital in Virginia where Cardiac surgery was not done but I would be responsible for teaching in General and Thoracic surgery and unfortunately possible duty at sea on an aircraft carrier.

So, by early Fall we were settled in a nice rented townhouse in Norfolk. Before leaving Washington, however, we decided to get married. So, at a Justice of the Peace with a few family members present we became legal. All was good even without going to California.

We visited both our families, during late Fall with quick trips to Pennsylvania and Milwaukee which fulfilled obligations. I liked the residents and staff at Portsmouth except for our Chief who was simply not a very pleasant man. But I towed the line as best I could. I also hooked up with the Norfolk Rugby Club which was a good outlet.

In December, D.W. gave me the exciting news that she was pregnant with a due date in early August 1981. Suddenly life was becoming very real, not just work, rugby and good times!

The next month, I got orders to relieve Dr. E. who was in the Indian Ocean on the USS Independence as surgeon for the carrier fleet. I would board the carrier while she was on a port visit to Perth, Australia. So, we made plans for D.W. to go to Milwaukee as I would be away until probably April. She would have the support of her family which missed her.

My route took me via civilian airlines to Chicago then to Los Angeles onto Hawaii then down to Sydney, Australia and lastly Perth on the West Coast. From Chicago to LA I sat next to a beautiful 35ish old woman which made the flight fly by. On arrival in LA she put on a full-length fur coat and we walked together a bit. There was a group of people protesting in the airport and as we got closer noticed they were animal rights activists. A guy noticed the woman's fur coat and yelled right in her face, "Do you know how many minks were killed for your coat?" I was prepared to intervene when she simply said, "Do you know how many animals I had to fuck to get this coat?" There was silence all around, she walked on and I stood there amazed as to what just happened.

Also, my old girlfriend B. had tracked me down from LA and asked to meet me on my layover. She was doing well, had many friends and ended up giving me an interesting send off in a lady's room. I couldn't resist – part of my testosterone problem. The rest of the trip was unremarkable.

When I arrived in Perth, the Independence was anchored off shore and I reported and was debriefed by Dr. E. My rank now was full Commander, so I had a stateroom to myself – small but adequate.

The three to four days in Perth were great as we had welcoming people, good weather and very good food. In fact, I discovered two great Indian Ocean fish – the Kingklip in South Africa and The Barramundi in Perth. Both fantastic but only the latter can be found in the states.

The officers of the ship were invited to a party at the Hilton Hotel and I can say that I have never seen more attractive women wearing alluring dresses in any one venue. Best guess was 250. The guys who had been out at sea became focused very quickly and the night was wonderful and my feeling probably sexually productive for many.

There arose only one negative incident for me. We were in a few bars the last late afternoon and in the last while playing pool the Canadian guy began insulting us and the USA. He would not stop, and I lost it, jumped across the pool table and hit him in the mouth with a cue stick. When he went down, we scrammed quickly out and back to the ship. And that in February of 1981 was my last bar fight.

We sailed Northwest the next morning and I began to get to know everyone and find my way around the ship. Two-three days out we found out that someone had a miscount of the Australians who visited the ship for tours as a young woman was discovered on board. She was sent back by helicopter and the sailor who hid her had the cost of the fuel docked from his pay.

We sailed Northwest to our station in the Arabian Sea (Gonzo Station) with another carrier group on Kermit Station in the South. Our medical group consisted of a Captain in charge (GP type), myself as ships surgeon, two flight surgeons (medical guys with special training in ENT and eyes) a medical officer, a nurse anesthetist, two PA's and corpsmen. My job was to perform surgery as needed and help with sick call. Obviously, there was a lot of down time interrupted by urgent problems or emergencies, training drills and sick call. There was lots of time for reading, writing letters, working out, watching flight ops, naps and the usual movie after dinner. One thing about letters – they needed to be numbered on the envelope because delivery on both ends was not consistent. One day a helicopter dropped a whole crate of mail into the ocean!

We only did a few operations as I remember; three appendectomies, one open ankle fracture with the aid of a textbook (then sent to Guam), some abscesses to drain, and one scope of a guy from a freighter which was food caught in his esophagus because of cancer. Otherwise we saw mainly problems associated with poor hygiene and other common stuff which I was not involved with.

We had three deaths secondary to accidents which brought home how dangerous flight operations were. Two young pilots were killed instantly when their Phantom fighter jet flew into the wing of another plane during visual flight rule maneuvers. The pilot in the other plane ejected and was picked up unharmed. The other incident involved a sailor on the flight deck that unfortunately stood up in front of a jet engine and was sucked in and killed instantly. Two guys who saw it happen along with body parts all over were brought to sick bay – I happened to be there to see these guys just staring wide eyed, shaking and sweating. The decision was made to put them in a heavily sedated state for a while then call the Chaplain. They were eventually sent back to Guam for mental rehab.

We had services for these men with remains buried at sea in a profound military service. The scenes have stayed with me always and I thought that only the relatives of these young men would know of their loss as we were not in any conflict.

We did have one very strange incident and one very amusing one. The former involved a sailor who was always trying to get off the ship with some mental problem, but the medical guys saw through this. Well he finally succeeded; this guy saved two buckets of his feces and somehow on a busy day got them and him into the cockpit of a jet. He smeared feces on himself and all over the cockpit! Volunteers were assembled to get him, and I watched this. He was throwing feces at the guys scrambling to get him which they did after the buckets were empty. What a sight! He was sent to Guam for Court Marshall with two Marine guards. The plane was rendered useless and simply pushed overboard.

I was told by one of the Marine officers that the guy had tried to escape in Guam and the Marine guards broke both his legs. However, my guess is that the pilots who flew the plane paid the Marines to make him pay.

The funny thing involved a Russian Trawler that followed us every day as a spy ship. The Captain got pissed off if it came closer than five miles and if it did planes dumped jet fuel on the Trawler and buzzed them. I went once on a helo ride with one of the corpsmen who brought a box of frozen hot dogs with him. They proceeded to "bomb" the Trawler with the hot dogs! It was really amusing as the Russians would try to catch them! Don't think the Captain knew about that one.

While at sea, President Reagan was shot, and things were heating up with the Russians in Poland. We were relieved by his stamina and quick recovery. Good work by a Thoracic surgeon I worked with at MCV who was then at GW Hospital in D.C.

We got a break with a four-day port call in Mauritius, a beautiful island in the Indian Ocean East of Madagascar. I had two plus days at a beautiful hotel on the beach and we enjoyed good food, vodka all day and a number of topless ladies. We were able to make calls home which was great, and we drove the entire island and explored. I met a very nice woman working at the hotel and she spent time with me at dinner and some intimacy on the beach.

We left the island to head back North a little worried as the situation in Poland looked bad with some reports suggesting a Russian invasion. Also, the Russian Bear reconnaissance planes seemed to increase.

As we neared the Equator it was brought to my attention that I was a candidate to participate in an old Naval ceremony where a pollywog becomes a shellback by crossing the Equator and enduring rituals and some minor abuse. It was actually a good time – we were led by ropes with grease on us through containers of foul liquids and water paints to a line at the end where each pollywog ate a sardine off of sailors greased fat belly thus proclaiming us shellbacks. We were then hosed off, allowed to clean and got nice colored certificates (which I still have).

We had one anxious time a few days later. As I was working out with the flyboys we went to battle quarters – the horn and then the words "this is not a drill" kicked us into high gear. I readied everyone in the O.R. for incoming wounded wondering if we would get hit by a nuke and be gone. We assumed that war had broken out over Poland but got no word until about one and a half hours later. A Russian submarine had gotten too close to our carrier force so helos with the ability to drop battlefield nukes on the sub were dispatched. Fortunately, it was driven off and we stood down. Many thoughts I am sure were in all of our heads during that time.

In April, I got word that I was to be relieved before the Independence sailed home to Norfolk, so I could take my Thoracic oral exams in Chicago. So, when my replacement arrived, I was launched off the carrier in a C.O.D. (carrier on board delivery jet) with one of our corpsmen. The funny thing was that someone had brought a cat to be put to sleep to sick call but since we were going to Diego Garcia, we took the cat in a carry-on sports bag to set him loose there. It was a sight when we launched – zero to air speed in about three seconds. The cat was looking out of the bag, threw his paws up, mouth open and hair raised. Too bad that we had no camera. Might have been the first time a cat had a cat shot.

On the island which was an airbase and sub base I had a day to chill out, relax and snorkel some. Then I was put in charge of the guys on the plane for the flight home. We took off from the island with brief layovers in Kenya in East Africa, Athens in Greece, Rota in Spain at our airbase and then across the pond to Norfolk and home. I do not remember whether we gained a day or two, but it was a long haul with no frills. My wife now obvious with child met me at the airfield in early evening and a hug and a kiss never felt so good. A day later I was back to work. I flew to Chicago to take my oral boards and passed with no problem.

I settled into a routine and also did most of the housework as D.W. was getting close to delivery by the end of July. On August 7, 1981 our first child, a boy, Colin Michael was born at high noon at Portsmouth Naval Hospital. He was delivered by natural birth with the great help of the British Commander who was a midwife. All was well and the exciting news was spread around.

We settled into caring for Colin and working when I had to leave again in October. This time I was ordered to have a surgical team on standby for President Reagan who would be attending an Economic Summit in Cancun, Mexico. My guess is that I was recommended by Dr. B.A. who operated on Reagan at George Washington Hospital and who was familiar with me from Virginia. I never found out. I picked my team, were briefed by the President's personal physician and the Secret Service detail. We were flown from Norfolk to Key West, Florida and were met by a Marine helo which promptly took us to the USS Shreveport sailing to Cancun in the Gulf of Mexico. This was a landing amphibious assault ship. It did have a nice operating room which we hoped not to use. We readied everything when we got to Cancun and then just stayed prepared on the ship until the Summit was completed.

When the President left with no need for our services, we were given two days ashore. My O.R. tech and I decided to rent a car and drive to the Mayan site at Chichen Itza in the middle of the Yucatan. We set out after a night at the hotel in Cancun and on the way laughed about how one of the Shreveport officers intervened and aborted a fight between some Marines and hotel security. Apparently, they thought the bill of food and booze was way too high and one Marine simply ate the bill! Security quickly came, and it was only the fluent Spanish and negotiation skill of the officer that avoided a giant melee in the hotel – the manager settled for half the bill so everyone was apparently satisfied.

We had a great visit to Chichen Itza. Fascinating history with remarkable well-preserved structures. We stayed in a small hotel, the only one there after many hours in the sun. They had a beautiful pool and we were there with beers when out came two lovely women with minimal bikinis diving into the pool. We obviously made contact with them discovering that they were British covering the summit for BBC News. They agreed to have dinner with us and my O.R. tech was already thinking ahead mostly with sexual intentions. Dinner was great and the company very interesting, but their body language and comments led me to believe that they were far more than friends. Well, I finally asked politely, and they admitted they were lovers for a while now. By that time unfortunately the bar had closed, we were thanked with a peck on the cheek and they were off to accommodate each other. I laughed as R., my tech, said that we should have asked if we could watch! I was simply thinking this – what would the Vegas odds be of two U.S. sailors meeting two British lesbians in the middle of the Yucatan Peninsula?? Life is interesting. Some days you eat the bear and some days the bear eats you.

In the morning we got back to the ship, shared our story which went all around the ship and sailed back to Key West where I and my team were dropped off to fly back to Norfolk.

It was good to get back home and relax with D and baby Colin. Other than me dropping him once from the changing table (no harm) all was quiet. Family came for Christmas and all was good.

1982 arrived and yet again I was out to sea on the Independence for workups in the Caribbean three weeks in January and three in February. A nice two day visit to the Bahamas with a fine party at the Ambassadors home was a highlight. It was great until I said to another officer there that the young woman, we were admiring was so beautiful that I would make love to her under a glass box at the Pope's funeral. An Admiral in front of us turning around, told us that it was his daughter we were alluding to and it was time for us to leave. We left, quickly. Another evening shot.

During these workups we spent time around Guantanamo Bay our base in Southeast Cuba. I was allowed to go over for an afternoon to visit but at the base were two nurses I worked with at Bethesda. We had a short but nice visit. Very stark base with no frills. Large protective fences with maybe half a mile of no man's land outside. Not a place I would want to be stationed.

Early April arrived, and I was gearing up for discharge in June. Dr. A. and another staff member had left the Navy in retirement to start a cardiac program in Reading, PA. Dr. M.W., another surgeon, and I were called to Washington to see if we wished to head up the Bethesda program in CT surgery. After much discussion mainly about people we wanted with us and other concerns, the Navy was unable to accommodate us to our satisfaction. I looked at a job with Dr. A. and also with the private group I worked with in Milwaukee.

After much thought and discussion with D, I gave in to her and rather than return to my roots in Pennsylvania we would go to Milwaukee and her family.

Before that, however, I was not done with the ocean. I was ordered to take another team for President Reagan for his Easter vacation at the actress Claudette Colbert's home in Barbados. This time we sailed on the Shreveport from Norfolk South. I spent a lot of time sitting at the bow of the ship reading. I learned that between St. Thomas and Puerto Rico we sailed over the PR Trench, the deepest part of the Atlantic Ocean, at 25,000 feet. We anchored off Barbados for an uneventful visit and a nice Easter sunrise service and a tour of the President's helicopter.

I talked my way onto Air Force Two for a ride back to Washington. That was a real treat – my own stateroom, anything at all to drink, steak and great wine and interesting people. That all came to an end on arrival to Andrews Air Force base. I was on my own to get a military hop to Norfolk.

So now, we as a family, prepared for a new life in private practice but in familiar territory. We said our goodbyes to a lot of good people. I would have many fond memories of my military service and I have tremendous respect for those who serve. These four years reinforced my belief that people working together for a common cause and superb discipline can accomplish anything. It gave me a strong love of our country and what our military does – we fight abroad so the folks at home don't need to defend America on our shores. We fight for one another, never to take land but to liberate souls and rebuild their land. We do not take home anything not belonging to us and we leave behind many Brothers in foreign fields with a white cross or Star of David above them. This sense of duty, honor and country I have always tried to pass on to my children each day.

June 1982 – 2000
We set out for Milwaukee in late May of 1982 with plans set up to look at houses along the North Shore suburbs of the city primarily because of the schools and stable neighborhoods. After a short time

with relatives we had our own home in Shorewood on a nice street with the only downside a mortgage at 18% (VA loan) the best we could do at that time.

All went smoothly with my restart with the Mayfair Thoracic Group and with a significant higher income we were able to make our new home very comfortable. This was important as we found out in late October that D.W. was pregnant with our second child!

I plunged into work getting back into cardiac work which I had not done in 15-16 months but that proved to be no problem with the help of my partners, Drs. K., R. and J.J. D. was happy with taking care of Colin, preparing for the new child and reuniting with her family.

For the first time in my life I was now in a stable socio-sexual situation with one woman with a family and a real job. Different, yes! How it would all work out, however, I had no idea except I felt that I will do my best to have a smooth ride!

The next years were full of making the house comfortable, adding on, the birth of our daughter D. and another son, R., many great trips to places like Hawaii, Bermuda, Kiawah, St. Bart's and Jamaica. There were many family happenings and just everyday interactions with the community. My practice was busy, lucrative and without problems allowing us a very nice lifestyle. I grew closest with Dr. J.J. who did all thoracic surgery not cardiac and we became good friends as well as colleagues. He knew everything there was to know about general thoracic surgery and this great always well-dressed man loved his motto of "every day is a business day".

Unfortunately, as in every life, there were tragedies to deal with. My brother-in-law, John, developed malignant melanoma in his early 30's. My opinion was that it was initially and then again not treated aggressively enough, and he developed metastases. I had offered prior to that to take him to Richmond where Dr. N. my former colleague could offer him the treatment he really needed.

He refused, saying he trusted his surgeon in Milwaukee. Before he became beaten down I took him with me to New Orleans January 1, 1983 and we watched Penn State defeat Georgia in the Sugar Bowl to win the National Championship. We partied with the team in to next morning and I will only say that it was a "Full Monty". John died in the spring.

While my parents were visiting us in September of 1983 my father had a cardiac arrest early in the morning. I was able to do CPR, place a breathing tube and revive him in our home. We got him to the then Columbia Hospital nearby and with a good cardiologist made all attempts to save his life but were unsuccessful as he had a major heart attack. I was beyond devastation, having failed. But I remained calm for my mother, sister and brother, made all arrangements for the funeral in Pennsylvania. The flight with my father's body in the cargo hold, all of us numb, was the worst event in my life thus far. I got through the funeral with difficulty. My father had worked hard to provide education for his three children and love and support and I wanted to do the same for my children.

I felt a downside however as even though D. never really became close to my parents, for reason never made clear to me, I thought that I would get more support from her, but over the ensuing weeks I realized that there would be nothing. On top of that my mother basically gave up, refused mitral valve surgery to solve her problem with moderate risk and died three years later. This, I had prepared for, so the event was much different but also a great loss of a mother who did everything to help her children grow up well.

After the deaths of my parents, especially that of my father, I had a hard time finding joy in life. All became regimented and mundane and really a chore not an experience. D. did not help me but perhaps I also did not really express my feelings and ask for help.

I filled my time with activities with the kids, my work and meetings occasionally away and being still involved in rugby as a referee.

I kept in good shape running almost daily and getting that escape on Saturdays in the fall and spring. Only occasionally did I laugh; times in the operating room when nurses asked me about "stories from the past, like getting shot at". And I always smiled remembering on early evening in late spring when my route took me past a small park where gay men hung out and as I ran by a few sitting on a table yelled out in unison "nice ass".

Then came a gradual turning point which ended up changing our family forever. K.M., a nurse at one of the hospitals, asked me one day to have coffee after work as I looked sad and maybe some talk would help. She was comfortable, easy to talk with and very easy to look at as she could have been a double for the movie actress Kim Novak. She listened carefully to all of my problems starting with the death of my father and asked good questions making me think about why I was in such a hole and how to climb out. Slowly this happened but it came with a cost as I became romantically and sexually active with K. It was too easy, and I should have stopped it but I could not. I lied to D. in order to spend time with K. using work, later meetings and even rugby trips to referee around the Midwest. Even once to Bermuda at the invitation of the Bermuda Police Club. How the hell I pulled all of this off is still a mystery to me as it was a whirlwind.

I felt a great affinity for K. as she helped me a great deal, had a great sense of humor and her lovemaking was both comforting and exciting.

However, my sense of family and sense of fidelity to D. began to take over and I decided to completely unmask the affair as it was already beginning to in itself.

Needless to say, this did not run an easy course. The children were still young, so nothing was said to them. D. and I decided to begin an intensive round of marriage counseling and complete honesty in an effort to save the marriage. I put renewed energy into the practice, doubled the efforts with the children and spent as much time with D. as possible. Initially things went well, or so I thought.

Meanwhile a crisis was brewing in how our practice was to be run with a new guy coming in, and who was to do what and where. Kind of an old-fashioned turf war. I was approached by Dr. B. a cardiac surgeon who had worked with a very prominent surgeon, Dr. J., about joining him as a two-man partnership. After weighing everything possible and writing down pros and cons I decided to join Dr. B. So, after three months of notice given it was another new adventure offering some relief from trying to save a marriage.

With the new practice taking me away from the hospital where K. worked and D. and I doing both individual and together counseling I thought that things were getting better. D. and I actually had two sexual encounters of her arranging that went well. However, those and other things turned out to be "tests" as she said.

In March 1992 D. simply said one evening that the marriage was done, please move out as soon as possible and nothing more. I found myself taking it very hard for far too long. The next day telling the kids, now 11, 9 and 5 that a divorce was now certain was worse than the day my father died. Colin said, "not you guys too" and it burned in my mind for a long time.

Now it was a process for two lawyers to work out as Wisconsin was a marital property state with all assets and debts split 50-50. Child support payments were set by percentage. I tried to mainly focus on the kids and my job. I found a nice apartment and we worked out schedules. The process was more difficult then I expected and took until September of 1993, 18 months. During that time, I took the kids to learn to ski in Colorado in February of 1993 and later in early September Colin (12) and I toured Central Europe. While there and driving through the Alps to Northern Italy from Austria we stopped for the third time for pictures. But Colin stayed in the car and then said, "You know dad, you've seen one Alp you've seen them all." Funniest thing he ever said!

The divorce was final late September of 1993 and my lawyer got me family support to pay instead of "child support" so it was tax deductible to me. All else was split. I got the land we bought on Kiawah Island, SC and D. the house. I eventually bought a nice townhouse nearby so the kids would be close and comfortable.

There were one two things financially I detested about the divorce; 1. The amount of money I gave D. each month was more than enough for three children but no account of it over what would be normal was required. Not fair. 2. We planned to give each of the children four years of college paid for, no loans. When I proposed to D. that we set up she said, "No! I will never use one penny of my money to educate our children. That's your problem." I never forgot that, but I kept the promise and did it myself. And that is all I have to say about that.

I continued to see Susan, the psychiatrist and counselor and learned from her that I had been caught up in a great river of life with D. commanding the raft. She told me it was her opinion that even if there was no affair D. had a plan of two children (the third not expected), accumulation of some wealth and then to go on her own. Apparently, it had lot to do with the complicated life with her father that "wowed" me but learning that she had a male "friend" in Arizona, was into mystical stuff and seemed well prepared for a divorce, it was all possible. Overall, it doesn't matter – I just had to find a new way forward with my children and not dwell in the past.

So, I did. I worked, met some interesting women and had great times. I traveled to Kiawah with the kids and I hiked in Acadia on the Coast of Maine by myself.

After almost two years, I felt better about the future. In August of '95 Danielle (12) and I had a great trip starting in Switzerland and ending in Rome. A highlight was getting a tour of the headquarters of the French Foreign Legion in Arbauge, France. The tall, French Moroccan Major was like right out of a movie complete with an eye patch. Danielle ran into her hairdresser in Florence and people she knew in Monaco.

Life goes on – Highlights of the next five years;

1. Forgot to mention that I remained good friends with my In-laws and saw them often.

2. Great times with and without the kids – St. Thomas where I spent a few days with J.L. from Navy days – wonderful sun and sex. Kiawah, Maine, New York.

3. One great Thanksgiving with my sister and family and brother, wife and my nephews.

4. Broke off with J.B. went on my own to work in '97 (fiscal reasons) then two of us back together and two other guys three years later.

5. Trip to Australia with Ryan (12) but then he got homesick up on the Great Barrier Reef and we cut short the trip.

6. Built a home in Kiawah – all decisions myself – not complicated – heard horror stories of spouses arguing over stuff like door pulls and knobs!

7. I began, in 1999, an interesting relationship with D.Y., an attractive, smart, sexy younger woman. She worked in hospital administration and on-air part time at a local country radio station. It was, at times, a bit crazy – sexual encounters of all

types at the beach, a restaurant, the Charleston Marina to name a few.

8. Colin chose Bucknell University in PA for college. He was doing well and played rugby with his size at 6'6", 250 lbs. They also had another guy from California his size and they were dominating. It was neat to get to referee one of their matches. Danielle was looking at colleges having worked on the Appalachian Trail and snowboarded on Mt. Hood in Oregon. Ryan now was only one left for child support and D. opted out of any fight for alimony, so the financial situation eased.

Getting into 2001 life was indeed interesting – it ebbed and flowed and changed in ways, but some things never would especially the love for my children and my promise to help keep them well.

Years 2001 through 2011

1. My practice continued with the only real change being my transition away from cardiac work except for assisting, devices and pericardial work. A lot of thoracic cancer surgery and some trauma and major infections was time consuming. The continued decline in Medicare (65% of practice) reimbursement rates took a toll in our salaries but we did the best to adjust. Also, we saw the beginning of "corporate medicine" and what is was to bring.

2. My relationship with D.Y. continued but seemed strained as I resisted another marriage and my commitment to the kids was also a major problem as she felt that she always came last. I enjoy her company and the relationship, and she is a great

traveling companion and lover, but I have no idea right now if I can make it permanent.   An old saying in Pennsylvania…" Once yes, twice maybe, three times, never!"

3. 9/11/2001 on a beautiful blue-sky day all over the USA the world turned upside down with the terror attacks in New York, the Pentagon, and a tranquil field in southwestern Pennsylvania. Everything changed and our country since then has been a war of terror large and small in some of the worst shitholes on earth. Unlike Vietnam we have supported our military as this was like a horrible strike at the fabric of our free life.

I took part in an interesting discussion with four or five docs who asked me if I thought this attack could have been prevented. My answer was yes. How? Years before when Bill Clinton was president and the US Cole was attacked in Yemen and sailors died I would have proposed the following: The USA will set up an all-volunteer anti-terrorist hunter killer force with all nations free to contribute with all persons fully vetted. The task force would be given the best of all resources with the assignment of going anywhere to find known terrorists, get all possible information if captured, then kill them. No one is to be brought back for trial. This would have been a monumental task, breaking more than a few "rules" and require amazing leadership but if the free world would have said enough is enough back then, perhaps history would not have had to record 3000+ innocent lives lost. Everyone alive today must visit the memorial in New York City. Sit and read this on a wall in massive letters: "NO ONE DAY SHALL ERASE YOU FROM THE MEMORY OF TIME" – Virgil.

4. Forgot to mention that I had a great New Year's Eve party to usher in 2000 at the new Kiawah home. Family, friends and relatives were there but also some were kept at home because of the Y2K computer scare that never happened. We loved the home, but the street became busier and visitors to the island would actually come up the driveway to look. The guy next door rented his home out a lot and someone who was a real jerk started building a home in front of mine on the beach.

It was ugly with stone cherubs on the deck! One night at a party we had we got modeling clay and Gorilla Glue, made penises and put them on the cherubs. Fun! So, I began to look at houses more secluded, found one and sold mine ending up well – paid the mortgage to build off, one million cash for the new home and had some money left over. Then worked gradually on putting my label on it with improvements.

5. The kids: Colin graduated from Bucknell and with the help of my good friend F.W., who was the Reporter of Decisions (Editor) at the U.S. Supreme Court, got a job in the Marshals office them became personal aide to Justice Souter then later paralegal work for a major D.C. law firm. He met Sarah, a health care attorney, and they were married in 2010 at a beautiful hotel near the White House.

Danielle attended and graduated from the University of Colorado in Boulder and by 2008, after an internship in D.C. she and her boyfriend Joe moved to Boulder. It was interesting that she had to take a semester off because of marijuana use when now the whole state is legal – and the lawyer who helped her said that most of the faculty smoked it! Weird world – but so was Boulder – full of lefties and where the homeless lived better than a lot of students. When she finished, and I went to pick her things up at her apartment, I could not believe the rat trap it was, and I was paying!!

Ryan opted to attend the University of Wisconsin in Madison to become an Engineer. I wanted him to go somewhere else like Boston College or Boston University or Purdue as I never liked Madison and had bad feelings about him being there – did very well for a while then came an event that began a nightmare but more on that later.

6. Sibling update – my brother and his first wife (who later died of M.S.) had two sons. One became a very successful plastic surgeon and the other a low-key manager with Home Depot married with three girls. My brother had a successful career teaching and as head of guidance in a major northern New Jersey high school. He married just before retirement a wonderful woman (former teacher of the year) moved to New Bern, NC and traveled a lot. My partner had done heart bypass surgery on him back in the mid 80's and he had stents placed later and was now battling colon cancer.

My sister had a great international teaching career, then into the publishing business in New York. She married a successful businessman, former basketball player at St. Joe's in Philadelphia, and they had two children both now doing well. They settled in Norwalk, Connecticut.

7. All else – I sold my condo home in 2007 and simply moved into an apartment. This allowed me to switch my legal residency to South Carolina which greatly reduced my property

tax. Speaking of a tax, Wisconsin had a fee (1% or 2%) when you sell your house to go to the state. Might as well just take your wallet, it is theft! The Village of Shorewood made me put up the house number on the detached garage in the alley! I later wrote them a note saying I figured out why – it was to let the pizza delivery guy know where to deliver the pie to the illegals living in the garage!

8. Travels – D.Y. and I, in October after 9/11, visited my son Colin in London where he was attending the London School of Economics for the fall semester. It was just about the same complete with an occasional dead rat floating in the Thames. We arranged a tour of Normandy with a retired British Colonel, crossed the Channel on the Brittany Ferry and enjoyed an amazing nine-hour day. Col. W. was full of incredible facts and stories. Standing in the American Cemetery high above the beaches among the white crosses and Stars of David all facing west toward home brought me to tears realizing the sacrifice of many young men to defeat Nazi Germany.

We also visited my daughter a few years later when she was at the University of Barcelona in Spain. Amazing city full of culture, great trip to the wine country and the Pyrenees Mountains. Had to endure two children on the plane crying and screaming in Spanish from Madrid to the U.S.

Also had great trips to Mexico, St. John's and the British Virgin Islands (Virgin Gorda and Jost Van Dyke). A neat two places visited were the Islands of Collabra and Vieques off the East Coast of Puerto Rico. Also went again with my ex brother in law, Tim, and his wife to St. Thomas. There we did a bit of crazy adventure – rented a small boat and actually went completely around the Island of St. John. Got roughed up a bit in the Drake Channel! Most people thought we were nuts and I think they were right.

I had reunions with my old friends from high school in Colorado, the Jersey shore and Kiawah and a 50th class reunion in 2003.

I continued as a rugby referee until my knees gave out in 2008 and the after each one was scoped and cured I began as a coach of referees.

These last 10 years seemed to fly by with the combo of work, family, friends, my relationship with D.Y. and many travels. This left time only for sleep which many times was interrupted with thoughts of, "How do I make everything better?". All this was coming to and end in 2011 with the beginning of the downfall with Ryan, his near death and slow agonizing rise.

Before I move on, I must relate the story of my friend C., a story of an amazing self-made American. C. was born in 1930 in North Chicago. His single remembrance of his childhood was at seven when standing outside a woman's store while his mother shopped, he saw a black car pull up outside a barber shop two stores away. Three men with machine guns jumped out and shot up the whole shop. They then looked at him, he froze, they drove off and C. peed in his pants.

He never liked school and in 1944 at age 14 he paid the Chicago Clerk of Records $5.00 to issue him a birth certificate making him 17. He then took off from home and enlisted in the U.S Navy to fight in W.W. II. He served on aircraft carriers in the Pacific learning all he could about machines and making extra money selling his quota of cigarettes. He sat on a gun mount on the USS Missouri in 1945 and watched the Japanese surrender.

Upon discharge he found a job in Chicago eventually using his innate skills with machines to patent several machines for bulk mailing all kinds of mail. He started his own business in Wisconsin and "retired" at age 35. Two years after traveling the world and amazing adventures (in which I do not know how he stayed alive) he went back to his business and prospered. I met him in our local coffee shop about 20 years ago.

Now he is 88 and in fading health. His son-in-law runs the scaled down business, but his machines are still sold worldwide. This amazing man is a great example of what can be accomplished in this country with hard work, a great idea, and a bit of luck. Education is not always required.

Update Charles did pass away peacefully in the late Spring of 2018. I miss his advice and his great stories.

Spring 2011 to December 2017

Six plus very tough years in survival mode with a few bright lights…

The good – Colin and Sarah had fraternal twins, Skylar and Connor, and moved to new jobs in Pasadena, CA. Colin now had his graduate degree in International Security from Johns Hopkins. Danielle and Joe were secure in the Denver area, married and had a beautiful daughter, Sloane, in early 2017.

A contract was negotiated by us with Froedtert Hospital and the Medical College of Wisconsin for us and all of our employees to be employed as the Community Arm of Cardiothoracic Surgery. It turned out well for me especially as I was named Medical Director, got a little more money for that but had to battle the corporate entities. For the record, I won most of the battles and our people were grateful. This stabilized our group and the people who worked for us.

In October of 2015, my personal life changed in a dramatic way. Our high school group planned a reunion at Kiawah since we had or soon will be 70 in 2015. Because of historical rains off the ocean a number of people were unable to come. Stars aligned in their courses and I found myself hosting no one but Sandy in my house. Background required – she was one of our "group" in high school and went to Penn State with Frank, one of my best friends and me. I was too shy to pursue her in high school and she gradually moved closer to Frank.

They married after college, she had a career as an elementary school teacher and Frank in engineering and business (MBA from Stanford). They had two boys and moved around but ended up in Denver in 1983. I saw both at reunions of our group and with my kids when skiing in Colorado. I always admired Sandy as she was the kindest person I ever met. However, around 2004, Frank started what became a severe addiction to gambling. Sandy left him in 2005. I felt a great affinity for Sandy but my long tine friendship with Frank prevented me from any approach. In 2013 he developed bad oral cancer which eventually took his life in the Fall of 2014. I visited him the Spring before he passed, and it was hard. Also had dinner with Sandy, my daughter and husband. She was radiant. Sandy never divorced him and helped with his care until the end.

One night at Kiawah with an ongoing amazing thunderstorm and us alone I asked Sandy to sit down with me and tell me how all was really going for her. After a short time, we just spontaneously fell into each other's arms and enjoyed an incredible night of tenderness and exploration and simple closeness. I never felt such passion and hunger from a woman as I did that night. In the morning we were left to figure out…what now? I told her that I wanted to contact her and arrange a meeting six months ago, but I kept putting it off. I said now we have a great story to tell – huge rains, fate and lightning!

When back in our homes we talked and wrote which culminated with me spending Thanksgiving in Colorado and both of us having a wonderful time in New York just before Christmas. It was in the city late one evening that I told Sandy that I was certain that I was in love with her. She is beautiful, kind, smart, practical and passionate and I then knew that I wanted to be with her. We spent as much time together as possible; her first in person Denver Broncos football game in Denver, an exciting overtime victory over New England and she was like a five-year-old at Christmas! We did a trip to Kiawah, a long road trip visiting back east (2000 miles and we were still smiling at each other), and ten days in Rome and a great villa near Cortona in Tuscany. Somewhere along the line we agreed that we both wanted to share our lives together for as long as we have left on earth. That began the exploration of a plan on how to be together in the most comfortable and financially feasible fashion keeping in mind the commitments to our families. The adventure begins!

The end and the bad – In 2010, D.Y. lost her job at the radio station and after long conversations we had she decided to go to Kiawah, take care of the house and improvement projects and decide what to do. She did a magnificent job with the house updates as her background in purchasing and her keen eye for bargains and good workmanship helped me a great deal. I got down as much as I could but not as much as she wanted, and she put the gas on the marriage pedal again.

That came to a bit of a painful moment one time before we were to go to Charleston – again discussing marriage and not going well. I was seated on the couch and she got up with her long stiletto high heels, angry and after a few more words strongly put one of those into my left thigh – and I do not think she was aiming for my thigh! She them took off and that began a slow descent of our relationship to a one of just business. In the end, since we had such a long relationship with many good times, I gave her funds to get a piece of land on the Stono River off Kiawah and build a small house. She ended up, in the opinion of the design build team, wanting to build an $800,000 home on a $220,000 budget, lost $20,000 in the process but kept the land. She did not take my advice and eventually headed to St. Augustine in Florida and bought a small home near the ocean. I wished her well and kept in touch. Many times I wished al would have worked out as she wanted but I take full responsibility for the failure as I had not enough left after my family to sustain a good relationship.

One day in March of 2011, I awoke early with mild chest pain and felt this was a pending heart attack, got myself to the E.R. at St. Mary's nearby, got to the cath lab quickly and had a branch of my right coronary artery opened up. However, I had other blockages and my partner Dr. Mc.M. did a four-vessel bypass off pump with no problems. Basically, I should have walked out of the hospital in three days – but hold up!... as my mother would say…I paid for my sins! Interesting, because I had just seen my cardiologist, Dr. R., two months previously with good checkup and labs.

The cardiologist who did the catherization went through the back wall high up on my right femoral artery which cause considerable bleeding in my retroperitoneum and large drop in my blood count. Then the spiral began; home then back in with rupture of the blood into my free abdominal cavity, six units of blood, slow recovery followed by fevers in late May. Discovered to have an intraabdominal abscess because of the blood. It was drained by radiology who also earlier repaired the injured artery. Then six weeks of intravenous antibiotics, drain management and more recovery. By September of 2011 I was totally recovered but had looked at a chance of death by complication and I learned a lot being on the other side, believe me. I also held a grudge against the cardiologist as he never followed up with my course. I took care of that later. The powerful antibiotic thinned out my hair, left no taste to food and caused small cavities, which I never had. Just more bullshit to pile on to my plate, but I did persevere and paid for my sins.

Passings - I lost my brother in Fall of 2013 to metastatic colon cancer but at least saw him a few times before his real downhill slide. We had become close later in life. I also lost my good friend Frank W. suddenly from a cardiac event in 2016. He was the editor at the Supreme Court and we talked all the time. I also lost several colleagues and friends much too soon. I lost four friends from the same problem – glioblastoma of the brain.

The ugly – Ryan excelled in his first two years at the University of Wisconsin in Madison but then came the ugly – for years. His high school girlfriend T. went there also. In his third year she became pregnant, told Ryan she was to have an abortion, changed her mind and then told Ryan after the baby was born – a girl named Chloe. Ryan wanted to get married, work and eventually finish college but then they decided to give the child up for adoption which was successful with a nice couple in the Milwaukee area. I do not really understand what happened then as Ryan wanted to stay with T. but that was not to be. She rejected him and walked away.

Ryan completely fell apart such as I have never seen. His studies suffered, he became depressed and started drinking. Any advice that I gave did no good. We (his mother included) tried as much mental health and substance abuse out-patient care for Ryan as possible and he transferred to U.W. in Milwaukee. Nothing seemed to help, he clicked with no one and so after a nasty episode of alcohol withdrawal, he agreed to in-patient treatment at Cottonwood in Tucson, Arizona for two months ending before Christmas 2012.

The people there were professional and did a great job. Then came a decision which I very much regret. They recommended a halfway house in Colorado, but Ryan wanted to come home and obtain his degree. Unfortunately, I went with the latter.

For a while, things went well, and I was encouraged. He moved in with me, worked with an alcohol counselor whom he liked but then threw Ryan out of his care because he would not do A.A. and wanted an alternative. Then we had drinking again, a bout of pancreatitis, warnings of continued drinking given by docs and so forth. Ups and downs continued. Ryan did get his degree but had a very difficult time finding a job, but he did not give a good effort. Earlier on he had contact with the child, Chloe but gradually gave that up and I believe it played a role. The fact that it took him so long to graduate played a role too.

In January of 2017, on return from a short trip to Colorado to see Sandy, Ryan had drunk quite a bit, was obviously ill and I took him immediately to St. Mary's. He had pancreatitis which deteriorated to necrotizing size and septic shock.

Near death, we transferred him to Froedtert, the medical school hospital where two amazing surgeons Dr. C. and Dr. P. worked very hard to save his life which was only put at 3-5%. Sandy, Colin and Danielle came quickly and after a family conference Ryan underwent an operation to turn the tide. Incidentally, his mother initially did not want anything done but after a family discussion, she relented. I had his Power of Attorney, so the operation would have proceeded.

After the operation, followed by another, and with great care in the ICU and recovery of his kidneys and liver, Ryan gradually made progress. The fact that my sister had her whole church praying daily was a big help.

Almost my entire life, for 85 days at Froedtert, was consumed with this fight. Sandy was great and was instrumental in helping me through this ordeal. I have never been in such a high state of anxiety ever, partially because I felt that I had not done enough to prevent this tragedy.

In June, Ryan went home but had another two admissions the last one in November to clean out remaining dead tissue. This was successful and left Ryan with only one drain. Now it began the process of rehab, weight gain and recovery and mental recovery. Still a lot to do.

One thing I must mention that I went through during all of this was clear age discrimination. One of the hospitals we worked at somehow passed into their bylaws that any physician reaching 70 years of age had to go through physical exams and extensive cognitive examination to assure no evidence of dementia. This even if no evidence of dementia was presented. I did it as I needed to help my partners. It was four plus hours of incredible, at times laughable, and ridiculously hard testing. One game was, I believe, designed to see if you would tell the tester to go f--- themselves and walk out. The people who supported this project, which I passed, should be sued by someone. I had no time as my son was fighting or his life at the time. I did as in other instances send them a "navy letter" named so as I learned this in the Navy.

Example – it goes…
From – Me
To – Parties involved
Subject – In this case obvious age discrimination
1. F—K you.
2. Strong letter to follow.
Sincerely, (etc.)

Quite legal, and many times gave me a sense of a good ending and a sense of revenge. Next – time to move on in life.

January 2018 until Present Day

I made the decision in the Fall of 2017 to retire January 1st, 2018. The only place that I felt really good at work was my sanctuary – the operating room. I was in charge, enjoyed operating and teaching and the banter and comradery. Everything else (salary excepted) had hit bottom. As physicians we were now relegated to nowhere land in the new realm of what I call Corporate Health Care.

The majority of the administrators knew nothing about how to properly run a hospital with all its moving parts. They sat in their offices all day at meetings speaking their corporate language with the only goal being the bottom line getting better and looking great in the press. I saw this on too many occasions trying very hard not to throw up.

None of these people were ever seen in the places that counted with the people that counted asking good questions and looking at problems – the OR's, the ER's the floors and the ICU's with the people working their butts off taking care of patients.

I saw physicians with concerns being completely dismissed and major problems never addressed. For example, at one of our major hospitals doing cardiac surgery I brought up this fact at the division meeting; does everyone here realize that this hospital cannot do more than one heart surgery at a time? How can we have a program? Silence ensued, and nothing was done.

A very fine thoracic surgeon and fine gentleman longtime colleague who served Milwaukee for over 35 years announced his plan to retire in three months. The very next day his credentials were taken, and he was told to leave his office that day. Not a word resembling "thank you" was ever spoken. Disgusting is too nice a word for that action. My vote for the person responsible – a Black Mamba snake placed in the back seat of his or her car.

Basically, most of the people who now run hospitals are incompetent suits who only know how to run dog and pony shows. I think you get the picture. Most physicians now are employed piece workers who must tow the corporate line or be forced out.

I started out in surgical training in Richmond and everything was cutting edge, trying new treatments and ways of caring for patients in an exciting atmosphere. I went through the decades and saw the evolution to the point when I left as a thoracic surgeon I only had the operating room as my sanctuary to keep going. That wasn't enough so there are new paths to explore such as this undertaking.

When I am asked about a career in medicine now, I answer that one should chose it for prestige, money or lifestyle but rather because of a calling – a need to help humankind battle disease, help find cures and reconstruct lives. Realize that you will be, in most instances, an employee in a large corporate structure. You will be given a quota to make of money collected and patients to see. Make those numbers or you will be gone. The electronic health record will take over your life of caring for people. You will abide by rules and regulation as thick as the U.S. Tax Code and submit to constant review.

I hope that there will be points of light that arise – hospitals and clinics run by physicians and nurses in an environment of great competency, compassion, care and constant improvement. A place with good pay, respect and comradery where patients feel safe and confident and the staff is always asked how are you doing and how can I help. I would unretire!

Enough of that. We will see what happens. On March 1, 2018 after gaining stability with Ryan's recovery in Milwaukee and arranging health care in Colorado we packed our Jetta and, not looking back, survived the trip through Iowa, Nebraska and the 185 miles of Colorado prairie to Lone Tree, south of Denver. Sandy had sold her condo for a good price and we had decided on a new apartment complex with a nice view of the mountains on the fourth floor. I certainly appreciated Sandy's willingness to have Ryan with us to fully recover. We got everything situated then set in motion the adjustments to retirement while Ryan worked to gain full strength and mobility.

I must say that emergency, middle of the night calls and weekend hospital rounds were not missed, and it felt great to sleep in if desired. Having Sandy in my life full time has been wonderful in many ways and she had gradually begun to help me be a better person. All I can do is advise her on how to channel her thorough dislike of President Trump into something productive such as volunteering for a Democratic Congressional candidate. She occasionally thinks about substitute teaching again but quickly throws that to the wind.

I now have found time to write, read more, get back to some golf, reconnect with some old friends, workout more and have a midafternoon nap. I also contacted the Colorado Rugby Referee Society, was warmly greeted, and quickly put to work coaching and evaluating two or three times a week this past spring season. I will continue.

I obtained my Colorado M.D. license without any problem except for the online 200+ items to check or answer and paying one day $5.00 each 15 minutes to park in downtown Denver! I have been trying to find out who does what in the Denver area, any possible part time help needed including the V.A. system. Unfortunately, I have received no return calls from any surgeon in the private sector or academics. Even a call to say that there is no interest or need to talk to me would be helpful. There are still one or two leads to follow but I will not push far on this path.

I am seven months into retirement and have decided to do a full analysis of the economics in order to decide if it is feasible to continue to have both the Kiawah home and a nice high-end apartment in Colorado. We all face these kinds of issues unless we work until we drop. If the following had not occurred, I would not be doing an analysis: 1. Divorce as I lost half of everything. 2. The education of three kids, two at private universities and 3. The decision to finance a home for D.Y. Of course, if I had married J.L. instead of D.W. two and three are negated and one also, most likely.

Now the main issue is how to manage things going from a $300,000+ yearly salary to having about $105,000 yearly available. The Colorado apartment is not a problem as Sandy and I split the cost. She has a very healthy pension form Colorado PERA.

The Kiawah home is the big problem with three issues:
1. Home, hurricane and flood insurance is $8,500 per year.

2. Upkeep (including landscape care) averages $4,500 per year.

3. Home equity line for D.Y. home is $18,000 per year principle and interest.

Of note taxes are cheap at $4,000 per year. The above does not include cable, utilities and electric plus all the small stuff. So, after all my analysis I find myself short about $1,500-$2,000 per month. What are the options grandpa??

The Good, the bad and the non-starters...

Nonstarters - leave Sandy and Colorado and plant myself at Kiawah probably without Ryan. I love them both and right now we all need each other. Sandy would not leave Colorado for South Carolina full time.

Bad – Rent the house. Probably would need ten weeks to at least pocket $25,000+. My experience is that strangers do not take care of things and overall it is a pain in the ass.

Good – Possibility of having friends and relatives use the house for a reduced rate. I am exploring that now but probably a pipe dream.

...and the just plain what I HAVE to do – Sell the home for hopefully $1,200,000, thereby pocketing close to $800,000 after expenses and paying off the debt.

Seems like Econ 101, does it not? But it is difficult as Kiawah is a place that I really love. But having funds to travel to new places would be pure adventure – Israel and Jordan, New Zealand, Anguilla in the winter. Unless I win a lottery, the last option will be the only option. End of that.

On the family front my daughter and her husband and child are relocating to Santa Cruz, California for a great opportunity for Joe while Danielle keeps her job. My older son, his wife and the twins will relocate from the West Coast back East possibly to New England. They will stay at Kiawah for some time until they decide. They made a good profit on their home in South Pasadena and have skills to carry them anywhere. I will continue to work with Ryan to get him back into the game of life.

My thoughts now are to leave my readers with some reflections, hopes for our country, teachings and favorites…

All of my life I have tried to do my very best for those I loved, my patients and colleagues and my country. I truly believe that I have succeeded in various degrees in all aspects of life except at being a husband. I admit that this was due mainly to a weakness for women and a need for variety. Any other reasons are still a mystery to me and I have set that aside.

I have struggled most of my professional life as to the existence of God and afterlife. While young I went to a Catholic church often but later became more "Lincoln like" just as Abe held his religion close, he did not attend services, although I occasionally do. As a scientist and amateur historian, I have thought about Jesus and Christianity. I believe that, all else aside, Jesus was crucified by the Romans because Pilate was convinced that he was a threat to the Roman Empire as a rebel. His disciples were ordinary men, mainly fishermen. I have always wondered how it was that, instead of this new religion dying after the death of Jesus, what happened to send that religion like a furious fire throughout the known world fueled by his disciples who seemingly should have scattered. Was Jesus really the Son of God who arose from death or a man who somehow recovered from near death to carry on, advancing his principles from seclusion? I, perhaps as you, remain perplexed, but SOMETHING did happen. Thus, this last great mystery remains until we die.

I have left my thought on the state of health care in our country and will not dwell on that any more. All I can say is that if we do not reverse this corporate mentality, we will languish with many health care workers and patients wondering why they are, overall, ill-served.

My thoughts about my country now and what I would love to see:

1. Shrink the Federal Government down to what our Founding Fathers provided for and give the states more powers - in Washington D.C. our three branches of Government, the Departments of State, Treasury, Defense, Commerce, Homeland Security, Justice and the FBI. Leave such Departments as Agriculture and Education for each state to administer.

2. We need term limits for the President of the United State (maybe one, six-year term), Congress and Senate and the Supreme Court. Figure it out.

3. Spend no more than we take in from now on and reduce the National Debt with a National Sales Tax on everything but food for five years, then reevaluate.

4. Require two years of mandatory service to the country of everyone able between the ages of 18-32. Many options – military, service to veterans, Indian reservations, civil service projects and inner-city projects or civilian service in needed countries. If we do not do this, we go the way of the Roman Empire.

5. We need to do something to stop the next election cycle starting six weeks after we just put someone into office! Period!

6. Replace our ridiculous Federal Tax Code with a simplified graduated flat tax with no deductions at all. Just think, you could store a year of tax records in one envelope!

7. Civility, some humility and the art of compromise needs to be reviewed and rekindled in our government, at all levels and at all times.

We are a unique place on this earth wherefrom original colonists from a few European countries we have assimilated people from almost everywhere on the planet. This has never happened before and after a civil war which took a horrible toll but ended the ugly practice of slavery we have prospered and persevered.

All we need to do is put aside our petty differences, and work on the major problems with respect for each other. We are in one boat and it is called Earth and we may be alone in the universe. Let what you do in life echo in eternity.

My last musings before ending is whether or not there are carbon life forms of at least our rudimentary level of intelligence somewhere in the vast universe. My conclusion is yes, but because of the vastness of the universe there will be no contact unless some incredible new form of travel permitting life to survive the trip is discovered. Otherwise an exploratory craft sent to a promising area or where signs of life are picked up would require procreation, and the circle of life in deep space for perhaps decades. Would anyone be willing to participate? Under what situation would it be worth it?

Retirement: The plan as of now is to do my best to get my son Ryan on the road back to work and a full life. It will take some time. I will give as much support as possible to Colin and Danielle, their loved ones, and help Sandy with her role with four grandkids. I will make sound financial decisions in the future so that we can travel and enjoy new places for as long as our health allows.

In the end, I sincerely hope that I will have left a legacy of excellence in my surgical career, as a father, and grandfather, with my conduct with my friends and relatives, and as a Patriot who loved his country.

I truly believe that the most important aspect of life is treating our fellow travelers with kindness, compassion and a willingness to help when needed. For the most part, I have done that, but I do regret the times I may have fallen short. The last 72 years have been an interesting, sometimes wild ride and now I look forward to many new rides and hopefully 15 years or so of being able to jump on the rides. I wish my readers fair winds and following seas on the journey of life.

ADDENDUM:

Personal Lifetime Favorites and/or Memories as of 2018

People:
1. All signers of the Declaration of Independence 1776
2. Abraham Lincoln
3. Jesus of Nazareth
4. Gandhi
5. Ronald Reagan

Places:
1. Jost Van Dyke BVI
2. The Wild Coast of South Africa
3. Cortona, Tuscany Italy
4. Low Country of South Carolina
5. Arcadia National Park, Maine

Events:
1. The births of each of my children
2. 9/11/2001
3. The assassination of JFK
4. The fall of the Soviet Union
5. My unification with Sandy

Vacations:
1. Trips with my children when each was 12 years old
2. Big Island of Hawaii
3. South Africa 1979
4. Jamaica, U.S. and British Virgin Islands
5. Rome and Tuscany

Sports I Played:
1. Rugby
2. Football
3. Golf
4. Javelin throw
5. Handball

Favorite Sports Teams:
1. Penn State football
2. New York Yankees
3. Brooklyn Dodgers
4. New Zealand All Blacks Rugby
5. The "Miracle on Ice" USA Hockey Team

Personal Achievements:
1. Getting my M.D. degree and being certified as a Cardiothoracic Surgeon
2. Serving my country as a Naval Officer
3. Establishment of the P.J. Swank Sr. Endowed Scholarship at Penn State to help students in my home town.
4. Funding college education for my three children saving them a long-term debt.
5. Learning to become a better all-around human being.

Lifetime Do-Overs:
1. Pursue Sandy in high school.
2. Marry J.L. – maybe.
3. Take the job in Reading, PA in 1982.

4. In 2012, have Ryan go to Colorado after Cottonwood.

5. Get out of Milwaukee after 10-15 years – keeping others happy and forgetting about yourself is unhealthy.

To Visit if Possible:
1. A number of Revolutionary and Civil War battlefields from the Mississippi to the Atlantic.

2. Montana

3. Israel

4. Botswana

Memorable Sports Events I Attended:
1. 1983 Sugar Bowl in New Orleans where Penn State beat Georgia for the National Championship.

2. Red Sox – Yankees at Fenway in the 90's.

3. Late 2015 – Broncos over Patriots in OT in Denver.

4. Army vs. Navy in Philadelphia in the era of Army's "Lonely End".

My Five Best Films:
1. GWTW – Gone with the Wind

2. The Searchers

3. Zulu

4. The Manchurian Candidate

5. Seven Days in May

Best Music:
1. Elvis

2. The Beatles

3. Buddy Holly

4. Johnny Cash

5. Sinatra

6. Neil Diamond

7. Whitney Houston's Star-Spangled Banner (National Anthem)

Others –
- Best job or position – Prince

- Worst fear – not responding well in a crisis.

- Super power? – Travel to the past as an unknown observer.

- Most thought-provoking place visited – The Gettysburg Battlefield in the quiet of the early morning.

- Most peaceful – Alone, at the top of a mountain on the Coast of Maine.

- Most lonely – At night in my stateroom on a warship in the Indian Ocean.

Quotes:

Thomas Paine – "I love a man who can smile in trouble, gain strength from distress and grow brave by reflection."

Anonymous – "Life is not measured by how many breaths you take but by the moments that take your breath away."

Anonymous – "Close is a word overused because the only places it counts is at horseshoes and hand grenades."

Brave New World – You pay your money and you take your chances.

Upon a review of this journey by a good friend, I was asked were there any common threads in the women I had relationships with? After some thought I realized that there were; each was attractive, intelligent, fit and driven. All were very sexual in different ways, from quiet but delicious to wildly adventurous.

Sandy, however, has something no one else had - a great kindness towards people, always. Oh, except with poor non-attentive drivers.

Update Finally, I have great news! Ryan is almost 100% recovered, has obtained, on his own, a good job and is much more independent. An incredible achievement (perhaps a true miracle) from as close to death as possible to a chance at a new life.

ABOUT THE AUTHOR

Michael Swank received his premedical bachelor's degree from Penn State University and his medical degree from Hahnemann Medical College. He became certified by the American Board of Surgery in 1977 and by the American Board of Thoracic Surgery in 1981. He worked as a surgeon for thirty-eight years, retiring in January 2018. Additionally, Swank served his country in the military as a surgeon.

Swank has three children: Colin, Dannielle, and Ryan. He currently splits his time between his residence in Colorado and one in Kiawah Island, South Carolina.

www.ingramcontent.com/pod-product-compliance
Lightning Source LLC
LaVergne TN
LVHW011847060526
838200LV00054B/4219